To Pat McEvoy
A Yorkshireman who loves Ennerdale

Introduction and Acknowledgements

This book is by no means the definitive history of Ennerdale. It is simply a collection of bits and pieces put together in the hope that it will be interesting and informative for locals and visitors alike. I have tried to be as thorough and as accurate as possible but if mistakes have crept in they are mine.

The book would not have been possible without the generous help of many people, and I am particularly grateful to:

BBC Radio Cumbria
Mr Joe Bird and Mrs Mary Bird, Ennerdale Bridge
Mr George Bruce, Ennerdale Bridge
The Staff of the County Archive, Carlisle
The Staff of the County Archive, Whitehaven
Copeland Borough Council
The Transactions of the Cumberland & Westmorland Antiquarian Society
Mrs Ronald Dickinson, Lamplugh
Mr Stan Edmondson, Seathwaite
Mr Warren Elsby, Keswick
The Foresters and Staff of Ennerdale Forest
Ennerdale Parish Council
The Staff of Ennerdale Village School
The late Mr Bill Fletcher, Egremont
The Freshwater Biological Association, Windermere
The Friends of the Lake District
Mr Jeremy Godwin, Penrith
The Hardisty Family, How Hall, Ennerdale
The late Mr Jimmy Hinde, Low Moor End Farm, Ennerdale

Mr Stan Hughes, Mockerkin
The Ireland Family, Whins Farm, Ennerdale
Sir Thomas Jackson, Mungrisedale
The papers of the late Col. R.P. Littledale, Workington
Graham & Debbie Watson and Committee of Low Gillerthwaite Field Centre
The National Trust, Grasmere
Mr Harry and Mrs Ruth Nevinson, Kirkland
North West Water
William Rawling Senior, Hollins Farm, Ennerdale
Robin Richardson, Ulverston
Ian Scott-Parker, Carlisle
Rev. Peter Simpson, Ennerdale Bridge
The Vickers Family, Howside Farm, Ennerdale
The Vickers Family, Mireside Farm, Ennerdale
Margaret Vincent, Kirkland
The West Cumberland Times & Star
The Whitehaven News
Mr Dennis Wildridge, Workington
The late Charles Williamson, Ennerdale
Mr Fred Williamson, Ennerdale
Mr Tommy Wren, Ulverston
The authors of the numerous books of reference

A special thanks to Jean Thompson for laboriously correcting the manuscript, and to Liz Boughton for helping with research and for spending many hours drawing the sketches.

Contents

Illustrations

West Cumbria - from a 19th century Railway Tourist Map

Around and About Ennerdale

in the beginning ......

Many thousands of years ago, when the melting glaciers of the ice age were in the process of gouging out the familiar 'spokes of a wheel' pattern of the Lake District dales, a particularly sharp chunk of glacier, shaped like a plough share, bit deep down into the rock below that rounded pudding stone now called Great Gable and, following a course a touch north of west, carved out a long narrow furrow until it slowly wore itself down to an ice cube and fell into the Irish Sea at St. Bees Head.

Geologists will not be impressed with my simplistic explanation of how Ennerdale was formed, but what is certain is that the twisting, grinding, scouring action of the retreating glacier left behind a narrow, steep-sided valley some nine miles in length with a deep, two and a half mile long, elongated lake at its foot. Exposed to life-giving air, the new earth was the womb from which came grass, plants and trees, and fish were spawned in the cold water of the lake. In time, wild animals and birds found their way to the valley, soon followed by tribes of primitive man who, attracted by this abundance of food for their families and wood for their fires, built their circular townships in the valley bottom. Very likely these early dwellers would have given their settlements names, but few have survived and it was the Vikings, who invaded Cumberland in the 9th century, who left a legacy of place names like 'dale', 'fell' and 'thwaite' which are in everyday use in the vocabulary of Cumberland and Westmorland.

When compared with other Viking names, the logical interpretation of 'Ennerdale' ought to be 'Enner's Dale', perhaps in honour of Enner, a Viking chief who had chased the natives out and claimed the valley for himself; but, as ever, scholars and historians cannot agree, and there are as many fanciful interpretations of the origin of the name as there are ways of spelling it. Some say the name 'Ennerdale' is Celtic and is a combination of three words: Ean, 'water', er, 'upon' and dal, 'valley' and so signifies 'The Vale of Water'. According to the historian Denton, the Irish called the dale Eaner or Ar-ean and the lake Lough Eanheth, 'the lake of the fowls', from the fowls that abounded on the island. Other writers believe that another name for the dale, 'Ehen,' is Anglo-Saxon meaning water, and the river Liza that runs through the dale into the lake is the Anglo-Saxon 'lizan', 'to gather', and so the river is the gatherer of many mountain streams.

In old documents, Ennerdale is sometimes written as Enerdale, Innerdale, Eghnerdale, Enderdale, Egnordale, Eynerdale, or the romantic sounding Alanderdale or Avenderdale. From all these has evolved the now generally accepted Ennerdale, which, in any language, means 'a very beautiful place to visit'.

a little bit of history ......

One of the earliest references to Ennerdale in ancient documents is in 1308, when Ranulph Meschin granted to the churches of Saint Mary of York and Saint Bees the manor of Avenderdale. For some reason the monks parted with it shortly afterwards. It passed into the family of Thomas Multon of Egremont and was handed on by marriage to the Bonville family, until in 1475 Edward 1V pulled rank and ordered that :-

> *Thomas Grey, son of Elizabeth Queen of England, might give nothing for the fine to nine writs granting licence to the said Thomas and Cecilia, Lady of Haryington and Bonvyle, his wife, the manors of Egremond, Haryngton, Gosford, Enerdale, Kelton and Wodacre, and the office of bailiff between Eyne and Derwent and between Eyne and Dodyn in Cumberland.*

But Thomas, Marquis of Dorset, hardly had time to enjoy his compulsory purchase before he was arrested by Richard 111 in 1483 for high treason, and his lands were confiscated. For a short while King Richard was the Lord of the Manor of Ennerdale; but, if Shakespeare is correct, he would have gladly swapped it for a horse at the Battle of Bosworth Field in 1485.

After the death of Richard, the Manor of Ennerdale was returned to the Grey family and, on the death of Thomas's son, Thomas Grey, 2nd Marquis of Dorset, in 1532 the estate passed to Henry Grey, 3rd Marquis of Dorset and Duke of Suffolk, the father of the unfortunate Lady Jane Grey. Still a teenager when, as the innocent victim of court intrigue following the death of Edward V1, she was crowned Queen of England; only to be beheaded on the orders of the evil Queen Mary who succeeded her. As far as I am aware, Lady Jane Grey had the shortest reign as Queen of the land and Lord of the Manor of Ennerdale on record. She was only seventeen when she died, and I like to think that she would have loved the peace and solitude of her northern estate. Had she visited it and decided to stay, the course of English history may well have been changed.

Lady Jane's father, the Duke of Suffolk, was also put to the axe and his lands seized by Queen Mary and her sister Elizabeth, who indulged in a little asset-stripping and sold the manor of Kelton (now merged into the parish of Lamplugh) to Christopher Morrys, one of the grooms of the Queen's Privy Chamber. As a light relief from having objectors to her faith burnt at the stake, Mary tried her hand at land-grabbing and found she could swell the royal coffers by wholesale eviction of the inhabitants of villages in the south of England and putting the land out for grazing to the highest bidder. It was highly profitable but, when the Queen's advisers were misled into thinking they could try the same trick in Ennerdale, the locals refused to budge. For centuries they had enjoyed a right of inheritance in return for a pledge of service on the Border to protect England against marauding Scots. On the death of a tenant, the Lord of the Manor was bound to accept his son as the new tenant, or, if he had no sons, his eldest daughter. His widow was allowed half the tenement for her life, *'provided she live honestly and do not commit fornication.'* The tenant was equally tied and could not dispose of his tenancy to anyone he wished. He was bound by specific conditions and duties, one of which was to have a horse and a suit of armour *'for service on the Border on every commandment.'* It was a system that had worked well, and the tenants of Ennerdale and district made it very clear that, Queen's orders or not, they had no intention of parting with their rights of succession in exchange for an insecure lease.

The Queen's strong-arm tactics came unstuck when she attempted to evict the Patrickson family from Carswell How (now How Hall farm). Well-educated, well-heeled, and with a reputation for being quarrelsome and revelling in legal battles, they knew their rights and refused to be intimidated. When Anthony Patrickson died, the Queen refused his son the tenancy of Carswell How on the customary terms, and on 3 March 1557 she granted Christopher Morrys, her one-time Groom of the Privy Chamber and Lord of the Manor of Kelton, a forty year lease on:-

> *Carswell How farm, Woodside, Birkley, Redbeckclose, Riggside, the water corn mill, and fishing in Fellbecke and Broadwater (Ennerdale Water).*

But the Patricksons flatly refused to accept the Queen's ruling and Anthony's son must have chased Christopher Morrys down the farm lonning, for he does not appear in official records as having taken the farm over and the Patricksons continued to live there for many years.

Having failed to force her will on her unruly northern subjects, Queen Mary abandoned her land grab and when she died in 1558 her sister Elizabeth was proclaimed Queen, *'and the bells of the churches rang gladsome peals and the skies were illuminated with flames which were not the instruments of martyrdom.'* But the church bells had hardly stopped ringing and the celebration bonfires burnt out before Elizabeth began to look for ways of boosting the depleted royal bank balance and, like Mary before her, attempted to compel all tenants to surrender their rights and take a forty year lease on their farms. In 1560 she appointed commissioners to survey her lands in Ennerdale and persuade the tenants to toe the line, but they refused saying it was contrary to their custom. Perhaps deciding later that a show of respect for the Queen would not go amiss, the tenants made humble suit that *'if the Court of Exchequer would consider their custom and be a means to have the same confirmed, it would encourage them to serve willingly on the Border.'* Elizabeth was obviously impressed by the loyal petition and, cancelling a lease arrangement she had made concerning Croftfoot Farm and other tenements in Ennerdale, ordered that all tenants were to enjoy their tenant right as heretofore. The Queen appointed a Royal Commission composed of Richard Ashton Esq., Receiver General of Crown Lands in Cumberland, Allan Bellingham Esq., Anthony Barwise Esq., George Lamplugh Esq., and John Dalston Esq., to survey again the manor of Ennerdale; and in April 1568 they assembled in Ennerdale to devise formally all the customary tenants at the old rents and on the same terms. The Commission swore-in twelve of the 'Ancientest and Sagest Tennants' to declare the customs of the manor, and they were recorded in a legal document.

Elizabeth appointed the Earl of Essex to the office of Queen's Bowbearer in the Forest of Ennerdale, an ancient title for the superintendent of the forest who probably never ventured near Ennerdale, but it netted him £3-0s-10d a year (approx £3-04p). There were both red and fallow deer in the forest, and Graves (Bailiffs) were appointed to look after the management of the forest and the manor. The day-to-day care of the deer was in the hands of two 'walking foresters' who were paid a fee of 20d (approx 7.5p) and allowed winter grazing for sixteen sheep in the Fence. The Fence (now called Side Wood) lay on the south side of the lake, and in a Parliamentary Surveyor's report was described as :-

> *All that Parke or parcell of ffell ground commonly called or knowne by the name of Ennerdale Parke, fenced partlie with an old wall, and partlie with ye water called ye Broadwater (now Ennerdale Water), abutting at Balthow to ye South, on ye Broadwater to ye Northe, on Redbecke Close to ye West, and on Silver Coves of Birkemosse Coves to ye East conteyning by estimacon 320 acres more or lesse*

The foresters would not have been very popular with the farming tenants; one of their tasks was to ensure that the Lord of the Manor's deer:-

> *hath libertie to feed and despasture without ye said Parke or ffence in any of the grounds belonging to ye Tenants of ye said Lord or any parte thereof without let or molestacon*

The tenants of the farms at Gillerthwaite were so plagued with deer roaming about and destroying crops, they resorted to drastic action and ringed their fields with old scythe blades, iron spikes, and very probably the swords and pikes they were obliged to keep for defending the Border. The deer could jump in but when they tried to jump out they were impaled on the spikes.

Throughout the reign of Elizabeth 1 the Ennerdale tenants were left in peace but, after the death of 'good Queen Bess' in 1603, dark clouds began to gather again when *'one of the most courageous of women was succeeded by one of the least manly of men'* in the form of James V1 of Scotland, who ascended to the throne of England under the title of James 1. Hungry for money, the King decreed that since he was now King of both England and Scotland, the Ennerdale tenants were no longer required for service on the Border and so the basis of their tenure was null and void. He offered to grant freehold inheritance of their tenancies at a price of anything up to fifty years purchase of their present rents, and threatened that, if they refused, their farms would be offered to others. It must have been a worrying time for the tenants, but they had an astute leader in Thomas Patrickson of Carswell How, and on his advice the offer was thrown out. Luckily for the tenants, the threats of eviction were never carried out. What with Guy Fawkes and his friends caught trying to blow up Parliament, the unsavoury murder of one of his noblemen, and the ongoing religious intrigue in his court, the King had enough on his mind.

It was about this time that the Ennerdale tenants started a law suit with the neighbouring manor of Kelton, which lasted for nearly four years. It was probably deliberately provoked by the Stockhow Patricksons who, at the time, lived in the manor of Kelton and delighted in stirring up trouble between neighbours. The row had been sparked off in 1597, when some of the tenants of Ennerdale had walled off eighty acres of poor land in Ennerdale manor that shared a boundary with Kelton, known as Bennefell, Gavelfell and Middlefell. Claiming that they had always had a right of common pasture on all the Ennerdale fells as well as Kelton, the Kelton tenants sneaked in during the night and knocked the walls down. The Ennerdale tenants took legal advice and, at Easter 1608, William Littledale of Mireside, William Rawling of Laverick Hall, William Jenkinson of Crosdale, Nicholas Williamson of the Mereend, John Rogers of the same, and John Littledale of Routen, acting on behalf of the Ennerdale tenants, filed a law suit against Anthony Patrickson of Stockhow, (a branch of the Carswell How family), William Patrickson his son, John Robertson of the Leyes, Anthony Fox of the Gill, and other tenants of Kelton. When the case came to court, Anthony Patrickson, who at the time was the collector of rents in the manor of Kelton, pleaded that the Lady of the Manor, Elizabeth Morris (corruption of Morrys), and her ancestors had always grazed common pasture in Ennerdale but, some years previously, when the Ennerdale tenants had elected a jury to survey and fix the boundaries of the Ennerdale commons they had led a blind man, William Littledale, the father of the tenant of Mireside, along the route they intended the boundary to go and it was set down as he directed. For their part, the Ennerdale tenants countered that the Kelton lot had no rights in Ennerdale anyway, and when cattle from Kelton had strayed into Ennerdale they had been turned back and their owners fined. Giving evidence on behalf of the Ennerdale tenants was 92 year old William Crathorne, a yeoman farmer of Banklands, Ennerdale, who said that:-

he knew the bounds for he was at the riding of them in the Lord Marquis' time....the bounders of the commons moores and waistes of the said manor or forrest of Enerdalle begin att a plaice called Water Cragge nouke adjoininge to Crosedell becke and from thence up the becke called Crosedell becke to Mearegill ffoote and so upp the Mearegill to the Mearegillhead and so from thence lyneallye to a plaice called hight of Sadlemoore Knotte and from thence lyneallye to hearegilheade and so to the overpene of Midlefell and that these said severall plaices to be the trew bounders of the said commons and waists of the said manor of Ennerdale.

He confirmed that when the tenants of Kelton let their cattle stray onto the Ennerdale wastes, they were fined in the Ennerdale court and paid. Gabriel Iredell, Clerk of Ponsonby, aged 76, testified that::-

he confirmed the bounders given by William Crathorne. He was the Clerk of the Court held in Ennerdale, at which Henry Patrickson was steward, who impanelled a jury of the eldest men in the forest to try the bounds between Ennerdale and Kelton, who found them as above stated.

Ellinor Morrow, aged 92 of Soskell near Loweswater testified that:-

She had known Ennerdale common for 80 years. Eighty years ago she kept her father's sheep on the said moors, and then the goods of the Kelton tenants never came into the commons of Ennerdale to her knowledge. If they did they were driven back.

The case dragged on through a total of six public inquiries but, when the the case came for a hearing on 31 October 1611, the Kelton representatives never turned up and the Ennerdale men won the day and were awarded £5 costs.

The case must have cost the Ennerdale tenants a lot of money, but they hardly had time to recover it from their farms when, five years later, they were embroiled in another expensive court battle in defence of their rights. Still smarting from the rebuff he received when he tried to force his land-leasing scheme through,

King James decided it was time to blow the dust off the Ennerdale file and have another go at his tenants. James summoned them to London, but they asked for a deferment on the grounds that their leader, Thomas Patrickson of Carswell How, had died and his widow had lost all the papers. Meantime, they got wind of a proposal to lease the Manor of Ennerdale to one of the King's Scottish retainers. Worried about the effect it would have on their tenures, and determined to settle the conflict once and for all, they raised the money to pay a lawyer to fight James in the courts. James by now was not in very good health and died in 1625, but shortly before he died he granted the Manor of Ennerdale on a ninety nine year lease to his eldest son Charles, Prince of Wales. How the Ennerdale tenants reacted to the news about their new Lord of the Manor is not recorded, but they must have been overjoyed when the courts judged in their favour and ruled that they were entitled to hold their land by tenant right. On the death of his father, Charles was proclaimed King and Lord of the Manor of Ennerdale; but, when the country was caught up in civil war between the Cavaliers and the Roundheads, he fell foul of Oliver Cromwell in 1649 and had his head chopped off. Puritan and religious zealot he may have been, but Cromwell had no hestitation in squeezing the lower classes for money, and did very nicely out of putting Charles to death by invoking an ancient custom which required the tenants of Ennerdale to pay two months rent on the death of the Lord of the Manor.

Oliver Cromwell died in 1658 and was succeeded as Protector by his son Richard, but he was no chip off the old block and, unable to cope with the demands of office, he was forced out and the country run by Parliament until, by clandestine political manoeuvring, the influence of the military was undermined and the monarchy restored to the throne. Amid 'delirious excitement' Charles, the eldest son of the executed Charles 1, was proclaimed King in London on his thirtieth birthday, May 29 1660, but for a while he was more concerned with avenging his father's death than taking an interest in the estates he had inherited and, when he married Catherine of Braganza, he gave her the Manor of Ennerdale as a present. Unfortunately for the Queen, her Council took advantage of her lack of knowledge of business affairs and the fact that her philandering husband was involved in affairs of a different kind and, having leased the Manor of Ennerdale to influential friends, deliberately neglected to collect any rent from them. In July 1676 the manor, with the exception of the forest and mines, was leased for three lives to Charles, Lord Grey of Rolleston. He was also appointed *'keeper of the forest and of the deer and other game'*. When King Charles died in 1685, there was even less incentive to look after the Queen's interests and, without telling the Council, Lord Rolleston assigned the lease to Francis, 2nd Lord Hollis who, on his death in 1689, was succeeded by his son Denzil, 3rd Lord Hollis. All of them gave frequent assurances that they would pay the increasing arrears of rent to the Queen, but never quite got round to it. When Denzil died in 1694, Joseph Patrickson, or perhaps Thomas his son, of Carswell How, petitioned to be allowed to lease the Manor of Ennerdale; but Denzil's cousin and heir, John, Earl of Clare and Duke of Newcastle, claimed the right, and Patrickson withdrew his petition but requested to be appointed *'Bowbearer as he and his ancestors had been in ye said Forrest'*. He appears to have got the job but the Duke, after paying £50 to the Council on account for the manor and promising to pay the rest within fourteen days, promptly renegued and ceased further payments. About 1696 the Council let it be known they were looking for another tenant, but the wily Duke promised to pay up and the Council let the matter rest. A year later the Council wrote again to the Duke asking him to settle the debt, but he never replied nor was the debt ever paid. When the luckless Queen Catherine followed Charles to the grave in 1704, she had hardly seen a fraction of the hundreds of pounds she was owed in rent for the Manor of Ennerdale.

The Duke of Newcastle died without issue in 1711 and Ennerdale was passed on to his nephew and heir, Thomas Holles Pelham, Duke of Newcastle, who, like his uncle, does not seem to have been keen on paying his way. By now probably thoroughly weary of anything to do with Ennerdale, the Council seized it back and leased the whole lot, manor, forest and mines, to Sir James Lowther on the 3rd of January 1765. The term of the lease was for three lives, but the Crown eventually sold the manor outright to William Lowther, Earl of Lonsdale, in a conveyance that stated:-

> *in pursuance of a Warrant from the Rights Honourable the Commissioners of His Majestys Treasury of the United Kingdom of Great Britain and Ireland bearing Date the 24th Day of September 1822 .....two of the Commissioners of His Majestys Forests and Land Revenues for and on the behalf of the Kings Most Excellent Majesty Have contracted and do agree with the Right Honourable William Earl of Lonsdale for the Sale to the said William Earl of Lonsdale for All that Manor and Forest of Ennerdale.....and also one*

Messuage called Caswell Howe and the Woodside with 18 acres of land and one Mill called Overdale Mill and certain lands called Beckley and Redbeck Close with the fishing in the Waters called Fullbeck and Broadwater and any other fisheries.....and also that Park or Parcel of Fell Ground commenly called Ennerdale Park otherwise the Fence now fenced partly with an old wall and partly with the Water called Broadwater...and also that Privilege belonging to the Lords of the said Manor for his Deer to feed on the Grounds belonging to the tenants of the said Lordship....and all Rivers Streams Waters Tarns Pools Lakes Watercourses Hunting Hawking Fishing Fowling Rights.....and also all Timber and Timberlike Trees and all Spiers and Saplings fit and likely to become Timber and all other Great Trees and Pollards whatsoever growing...and all Mines Veins and Beds of Coal Lead Copper and other Metals and Minerals except Royal Mines of Gold and Silver...and all Quarries of Lime Slate and other Stone now being and which shall hereafter be found or discovered in or upon the said premises.....At or for the Price of or Sum of two thousand five hundred Pounds of lawful Money of Great Britain to be paid by the said William Earl of Lonsdale into the Bank of England

Included in the Earl's superb bargain was Carswell Howe, once the seat of Kings, but they were rather different Kings from the monarchs who sat on the throne of England.

the 'kings of Ennerdale' ......

In the early history of England Kings and Queens came and went, but for two hundred years, between the 15th and 17th centuries, the real "Kings of Ennerdale" were the Patricksons of Carswell How, the original name of How Hall farm, one mile from Ennerdale Bridge on the road leading to the site of the Anglers Inn. It was not that the Patricksons were of royal blood or laid claim to the English throne, or were even particular favourites of the monarchy. They were a typical English landed family who lived in turbulent times and had a taste for money and power, an aggressive ambition and a total disregard for anyone who stood in their way. Oddly enough for a family who it is believed lived in Cumberland for three centuries or more and had such an impact on Ennerdale, very little is known of their origin. In old records there are vague references to Edward 1 granting timber to Richard Patrykson of How, and there is a mention of a Hugh de Patrykson who fought at the battle of Hexham in 1463, and who was father to John Patrykson whose son William built Stockhow Hall, now a farm close to Ennerdale Bridge. John Patrykson had two sons, Anthony and William. In 1536 Anthony's son, also called Anthony, is mentioned in the valuation of the Priory of St Bees as one of the bailiffs of Copeland and it is recorded that he paid 20d to the Prior of St Bees for a light to be placed before the image of St Bega in the Abbey. It was a good investment for, on the 30 April 1540, good luck came his way when Henry, Marquis of Dorset, *'for good service to himself and to his late father by his servant, Anthony Patrickson'* granted him the office of bailiff between:-

> *Eyn and Duden and between Eyn and Derwent... and the office of custodian of the forest of Enerdall and conductor of all his tenants in Enerdall, Egremont and Harrington, for his life, and after the death of the said Anthony to such son of his as he may appoint for his life for the fee of £3-0-10 per annum.*

Together with a new spelling of their surname, it was probably the turning point that established the Patricksons as an important and powerful force in the Manor of Ennerdale, and they took every advantage of it. Anthony Patrickson married Frances, the daughter of Sir Thomas Swinburne, one of the Privy Council to King

Henry V111, and they had four sons and two daughters, Roger, William, John, Anthony, Ellinor and another daughter whose name appears to have been lost. This main branch of the Patrickson family spread roots that in turn spread more roots, until tracing them all becomes very confusing. Obviously keen to have their own farms, three of Anthony's sons left the family home. Roger took Stawbank, then in the Manor of Kelton but now in the parish of Lamplugh, Anthony was his neighbour a few fields away at Stockhow and John went to Weddiker near Arlecdon. William stayed at Carswell How with his parents and sister Ellinor.

At Carswell How (How Hall) there is an inscription on a stone let into a wall that can still be seen and states, *'This house was built A.D. 1566 by Anthony Patrickson and Frances his wife, daughter of Sir Thomas Swinburne, one of the Privy Council to King Henry V111'*. There are those who believe this stone is a copy of an older stone and that the date should be 1536. The argument is supported by the fact that Anthony made a will in 1555 and died shortly after.

The Patricksons of Carswell How

Sometimes spelt Caerswell - Keswell - Cassil - Carswet - Caiswelhall - Castlehow - or simply How

Ellinor Patrickson was a rebellious lady who did not take kindly to being dictated to by her family. She married her neighbour George Lamplugh, Lord of the Manor of Lamplugh, but when he died in 1589 she caused a bitter family row by announcing her intention to re-marry. It was not her desire to marry again that upset the family, it was her new boyfriend, Marmaduke Redman, whom they suspected was a rogue and only interested in Ellinor's money. Though it was continually pointed out that 'her suitor by way of marriage' was already supporting a divorced wife and seven children, was in debt up to his ears and owed more money than she was worth, the pleas were blinded by passion and Ellinor went ahead and married Marmaduke Redman in 1591. But there must have been warning bells as well as wedding bells ringing in her ears, for she settled her property so that her new husband could not touch it if he got into debt. It was a wise move. Perhaps she was ill, or it might have been caused by the shock of realising she had made a dreadful mistake, but, a few months after the marriage, poor Ellinor died and the slippery Marmaduke, desperate to get his hands on her money, brought an action against her trustees alleging that they had unduly influenced her. The trustees replied with an intriguing counterclaim for non-performance of his marriage contract. The case dragged on until 1599, when it was discovered that two years previously Marmaduke had been outlawed for debt, and his claim against Ellinor's estate collapsed.

Before she died, Ellinor had tried to arrange a marriage between William Redman, the eldest son of her husband Marmaduke by his first wife, and her grand niece Anna, the daughter of Henry Patrickson of Carswell How. But, having been prevented from getting his hands on Patrickson money, Marmaduke was determined that no Patrickson female was going to get her hands on his son, and young William was told not to communicate with the lady. Being a Patrickson and not used to taking 'no' for an answer, Anna went round to William's house and demonstrated her undying love by hurlings rocks at the windows; but the lad's father sent for the militia and Anna ended up in court for causing damage to property. A short time later, still determined to get her man, Anna paid another call on William in the company of a pair of hefty relatives, and perhaps it was with the help of one large chap twisting his arm up his back and another clutching his throat that William discovered he wanted to marry Anna after all. A year later, in 1600, *'Richard ye sonne of William Redman and Anna his wief'* was born.

Having taken over Carswell How from his father, William, the second son of Anthony Patrickson and his wife Frances Swinburne, also succeeded his father as bailiff of Ennerdale in 1557. But Queen Mary used the opportunity to strike a blow at the Patricksons for refusing to move in March of that year, when she had attempted to evict them by leasing Carswell How to her servant Christopher Morrys. She took the office of bailiff between "Eyn and Duddon" (the river Ehen in west Cumberland and the river Duddon near Millom) away from the Patricksons and gave it to the Earl of Northumberland. The Queen's revengeful gesture might have had a noticeable effect on William's income but it is unlikely he would have been bothered. He was on the point of marrying Frances, the widow of Thomas Leigh of Calder Abbey, and she had a substantial dowry. By an interesting coincidence, Frances was the daughter of Sir Thomas Wyet, a Privy Councillor of Henry V111, who, together with the Duke of Suffolk and the tragic Lady Jane Grey, once Lords of the Manor of Ennerdale, was executed by Queen Mary in 1554 following a rebellion against her in Norfolk.

Frances died in 1578 at the age of 56, and William died a few years later leaving Carswell How to his only son Henry, who strengthened the family ties with the Leighs of Calder Abbey when he married Bridget, the daughter of Thomas Leigh and Frances. In doing so, it appears that either he married his half sister or that Henry was born 'the wrong side of the blanket' as a result of his father's indiscretion with an unknown lady prior to marrying Frances. It may well have been for this reason that a proposal made in 1595 to appoint Henry as bailiff of Ennerdale was dropped. In 1604 Henry's two sons, Francis and Thomas, were appointed bailiffs of Ennerdale; but Francis, the eldest son, decided that the life of a country gentleman was not for him and left home for the bright lights of London, leaving Thomas to help his father at Carswell How.

Henry was a particularly agressive person renowned for falling out with his neighbours and, in 1607, sued William Rawling, a yeoman farmer of Ennerdale, for felling trees in Salter Close, near Kirkland. William Rawling argued successfully that the trees were not on Patrickson's land and it was none of his business. Not content to live in peace, Henry was soon in the thick of a protracted legal battle with John Hudson, the vicar of Harrington, claiming that the tithes of Harrington and Lowca had been leased to William, his father, by Hudson's predecessor. Henry died before the case had ended and, in true family tradition, his son Thomas took it up, and in true family tradition lost it.

Thomas married Jane, the daughter of Sir Lancelot Fletcher of Tallentire, near Cockermouth, and had two sons, Joseph and John. Thomas was another typical chip off the Patrickson block and revelled in legal disputes with neighbours. At the height of a disagreement he was having with several Kinniside tenants, he served them with a summons to appear in court in London, hoping that, faced with the expense of travelling to the capital, the tenants would give in. But they took legal advice of their own and outwitted him. Choosing a day when they knew Thomas would be out of the county on business, they arranged for the hearing to take place at Brougham Hall, near Penrith, and Thomas was so taken aback by the tenants' crafty move he abandoned the case. Furious at losing face, he launched himself into a bitter dispute with twenty Ennerdale tenants over tithe rents, and took legal action against them. But again the tenants got the upper hand. They refused to have anything to do with him and said *'in a most contemptuous manner they would never abide or perform any order thereafter to be made in the Court of Chancery concerning the said tithes.'* The tenants revolt and the snub to his authority may well have had a detrimental effect on Thomas's blood pressure, for he died in London on 23 November 1622, before the case was over. Together with Carswell How he left the farms of Monghton and Scalderskeugh, near Gosforth, and Skallow, Gill and Cockyn in Kelton.

In 1623 Thomas's widow, Jane, married Henry Featherstonehaugh of Kirkoswald, near Penrith. Henry enjoyed the view of the lake and the fells from Carswell How so much he tried to obtain the lordship of the Manor of Ennerdale. Word had got round that the King intended to lease the manor to Alexander Foster, one of his servants, and Henry Featherstonehaugh paid a London lawyer £20 to acquire the lease. But King James changed his mind about leasing the Manor to Foster and instead gave it to his son, the Prince of Wales.

Joseph Patrickson, Thomas's son and heir, was only twelve when he inherited Carswell How in January 1623, but in the course of time took over the management of the estate. About 1641 he married Catherine, the daughter of Thomas Salkeld of Brayton, and they produced Thomas, George, Joseph, Jane, Isabel, Catherine, Bridget, Mary and Martha. Joseph's brother, John, did very nicely for himself by marrying Bridget, the daughter of Sir Richard Fletcher of Hutton. Sir Richard had bought Calder Abbey, near Egremont, and it is recorded that "Mr Patrickson on marriage to Sir Richard's daughter became possessed of Calder Abbey." John only managed to produce daughters, Barbara and Dorothy and the unfortunate Bridget, whose marriage to Sir Timothy Featherstonehaugh of Kirkoswald came to a tragic end when, in a battle against Oliver Cromwell, he was taken prisoner with the Earl of Derby and they were both beheaded in 1651.

In 1648, their late father's lifetime of wheeling and dealing caught up with Joseph and John when Ellinor Woodhall, a widow, complained that thirty five years previously Thomas had deviously persuaded her to sign documents which gave him the ownership of her small farm. The brothers were hauled before a tribunal where they vigorously denied the accusation, and in his defence said that their father was well known in Cumberland as an honest man, and his memory was so dear to them they could not entertain such unworthy thoughts of him. Thomas, they said, had legally acquired the farm for the use of Lancelot Fletcher, late of Dean, who was at the time a minister in the Church and known for piety and integrity. The impassioned plea may well have left the Chairman of the tribunal with a tear in his eye and he swung the case in the Patricksons' favour; though the result might have been different had he been aware that Lancelot Fletcher was, in fact, a close relation of Thomas's wife.

Accustomed to power, and revelling in the popular, if unlawful, title of "Kings of Ennerdale," the Patricksons of Carswell How seemed invincible but, in the middle of the 17th century, the tide of fortune began to turn. Years of senseless and extremely expensive litigation, and the strain of the Civil War in which the Patricksons were supporters of the Crown, had taken toll of their finances, and in 1658 Joseph was forced to sell his wife's property in Hensingham and Brayton. A year later he sold Cockyn farm in Kelton, and in 1670 he was in such desperate straits he had to part with property in Salter as payment for a bill he owed a shopkeeper in Cockermouth. He mortgaged Ennerdale mill in 1671 for £200, but it was burnt down shortly after and, though he immediately had it rebuilt, he could not pay the premiums on the mortgage and it was re-possessed. Both Joseph and his son, Thomas, aged 23 in 1665, borrowed large sums of money from many notable Cumberland families and were plunged so deeply into debt their creditors foreclosed. John Lamplugh, of Lamplugh Hall, had stood surety for the Patrickson loans which, with interest, had quadrupled in size and, obviously fearing for his own security, he sued Thomas and seized all his cattle and possessions. Now destitute, Thomas was thrown into Carlisle gaol. Bit by bit, Joseph Patrickson's estate was sold off to meet debts, but even when friends came to his assistance with offers of financial arrangements to help him over his difficulties, it seems he could not resist the temptation to indulge in trickery. The Rev. George Lamplugh, the brother of John Lamplugh of Lamplugh Hall, agreed to pay Joseph and his wife an annuity for seven years and also meet a number of Joseph's liabilities in return for Salter Grange, an area of about 20 acres of land at Salter. It was agreed they should all meet at Carswell How to settle the final details, but hardly had the first cup of tea and piece of cake been passed round when Catherine, Joseph's wife and Agnes, Thomas's wife, insisted that they must each have a new gown for agreeing to the conveyance. Being a parson, George Lamplugh would have had to choose his words carefully, but told them as forcefully as a parson could that if they wanted gowns they would have to get someone else to buy them. The burst of hysterics that followed apparently lasted over three hours and could well have been a ploy; for when at last the hullabaloo died down and John Lamplugh went out to get his money from a saddlebag left on a horse locked in Patrickson's stable, the bag and money had gone. The Lamplughs promptly left, taking with them the title deeds of the land.

Thomas had the cheek to sue the Lamplughs for the return of the deeds but, by now, any compassionate thoughts the Reverend George Lamplugh may have had about turning the other cheek, or loving his neighbour, had worn a bit thin. He countered with a law suit of his own, and Thomas was outlawed for debt. A true Patrickson, there are stories of Thomas drawing his sword and chasing creditors and bailiffs off his property, but it was the end of the line for the 'Kings of Ennerdale'. Thomas died, almost penniless, in 1697, and his mother, Catherine, a year later. Joseph, the patriarch of the family, survived them both and died in July 1700 at the great age of 91.

The Patrickson estates were dispersed, and Carswell How was sold to Sir John Lowther of Lowther Castle, Penrith. In due course the house passed to Joseph Senhouse of Calder Abbey as part of a dowry when he married the daughter of John Tiffen. He carried out extensive alterations to the house, then sold it. In 1816 it was the property of Henry Birley, a Whitehaven industrialist, who sold it to John Dickinson of Red How, Lamplugh. The Dickinson family of Red How, Lamplugh sold it to the National Trust in 1950 and it has been maintained as a traditional Lakeland sheep farm, presently tenanted by the Hardisty family, renowned as breeders of Herdwick sheep. In recent times, the rolling farm land reaching down to the lake was chosen as a venue for the popular TV series 'One Man and His Dog'.

View from How Hall Farm

the parish ......

The boundary of the parish of Ennerdale and Kinniside follows a meandering course through farmsteads and meadows and up the fells and down the dales somewhat like the Great Wall of China. Which tribal chief or Viking warrior first decided where the original Ennerdale boundary was to be by sticking his spear in the ground at convenient intervals is not recorded, but his task was made easier by following the fell ridges that enclose the Ennerdale valley in a natural horseshoe. On the lower ground, the boundary would have expanded or contracted according to how successful the Ennerdale chief was in his battles with neighbouring tribes until, realising the futility of war, the chiefs agreed a dividing line between their territories and permanent boundary lines were established.

When the Crown eventually claimed all the land and succeeding monarchs divided it up and gave estates to friends and supporters for 'services rendered', Ennerdale and Kinniside were separate manors with their own Lords but, in the course of time, the manors were sold into private ownership, and for administrative purposes Ennerdale and Kinniside were merged into a single parish.

In 1609, when 92 years old William Crathorne of Banklands, Ennnerdale, was giving evidence at a boundaries dispute and declared that he knew the boundaries, *'for he was at the riding of them,'* it suggests that at one time the Ennerdale tenants held an annual ceremony of riding the boundaries similar to the colourful pageants with banners and horses that still survive in the Scottish border towns. The spectacle of a posse of locals dressed in period costume and charging through Ennerdale, mounted on horseback and waving banners, may gladden the heart of West Cumbria Tourist Board; but it would take exceptional horses and brave riders to negotiate a route that took in Great Borne, Red Pike, High Stile, Haystacks, Great Gable, Kirk Fell, Pillar, Steeple, Haycock, Crag Fell and Grike. The nearest thing to boundary riding these days is when skeletal athletes, dressed in brightly coloured shorts and singlets, compete in the annual Ennerdale Horseshoe fell race in June.

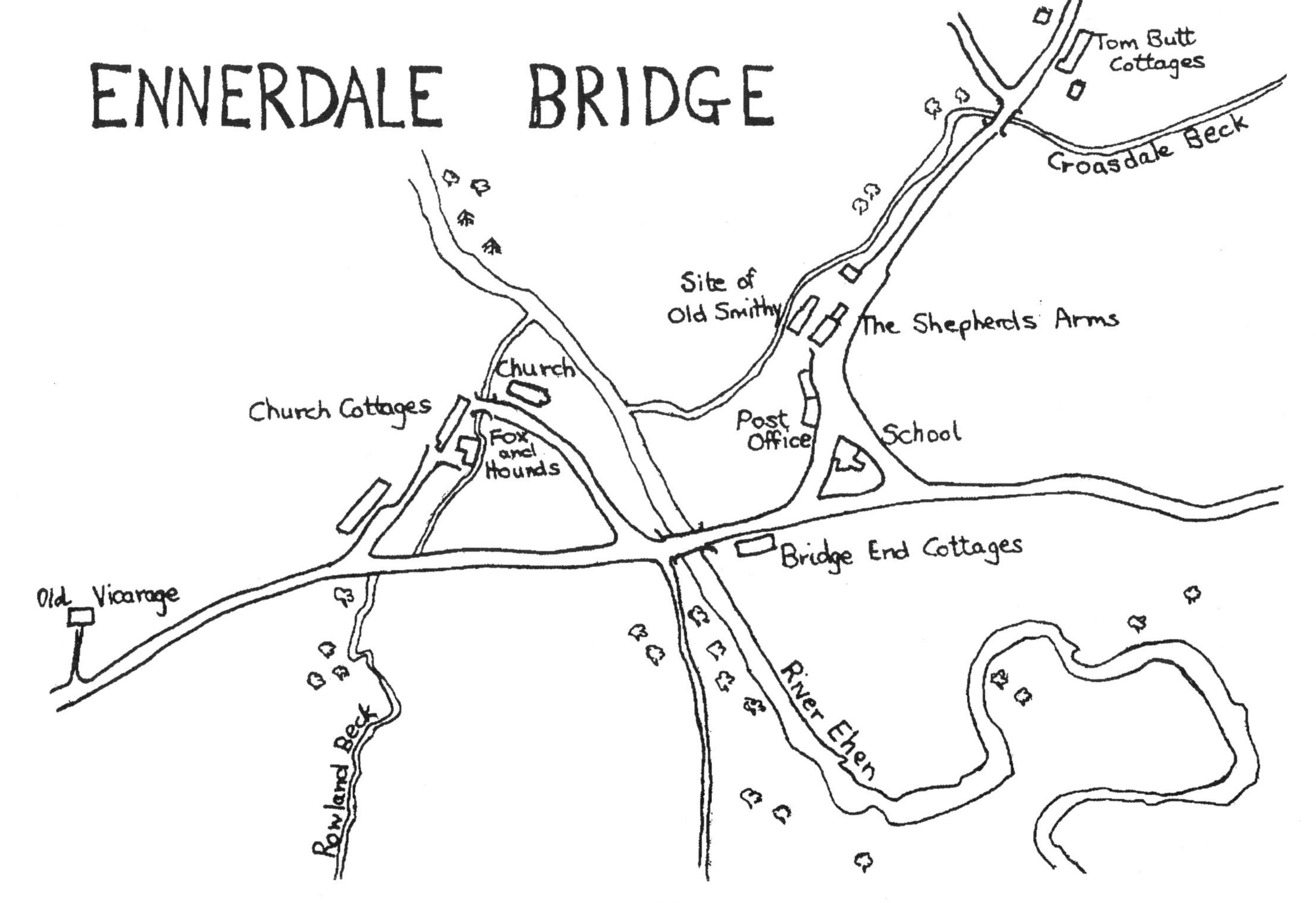
ENNERDALE BRIDGE
Tom Butt Cottages
Croasdale Beck
Site of Old Smithy
The Shepherds Arms
Church
Church Cottages
Fox and Hounds
Post Office
School
Bridge End Cottages
Old Vicarage
Rowland Beck
River Ehen

the village ......

After the Vikings built their first coastal forts in Cumberland in the 9th century, they gradually moved inland, making clearings in the old oak forests and establishing farms. The footpaths they trod between these settlements were gradually widened for the passage of cattle and sheep and, in time, became important highways. At strategic points along the highways, particularly where a ford crossed a river, people began to build dwellings, perhaps with an eye to making a living offering a service to travellers or to finding work on the farmsteads, and eventually a collection of dwellings increased to the status of a village. Ten miles inland from the coast, settlers were attracted to a sheltered hollow where a well-trodden path dropped down to a ford that crossed a swiftly flowing river at the foot of a valley. They built rough dwellings, pulled large boulders into a line on the river bed so they could cross without getting their feet wet, built a resting place for travellers, and, perhaps to save endless arguments at village meetings, named their settlement after the valley. They called it Ennerdale.

For many hundreds of years the village was probably no more than a few primitive hovels built of cobbles dug out of the ground and roofed with turf. Early 16th century records list about fifty dwellings in Ennerdale valley and village, but the number steadily increased and by the 17th century had more than doubled. At some time during this period of growth and prosperity a bridge was built across the turbulent and unpredictable river Ehen, alongside the ancient ford. Very likely it would be roughly built of wood and just wide enough to carry a loaded packhorse, but for the locals it was a considerable boost in status and they celebrated the occasion by renaming the village Ennerdale Bridge. It is possible that the bridge was soon replaced by a more substantial construction capable of taking heavy farm carts.

The development of wheeled traffic, improvements in agriculture, new techniques for quarrying local stone, and the harnessing of water to provide power, all contributed to make Ennerdale village an important focal point that attracted tradesmen and speculators like moths to a candle. But they had their share of problems. When the first Ennerdale village settlers chose a sheltered area with plenty of water available, they could not have anticipated that the river Ehen and Croasdale Beck would eventually mark the boundaries of three manors; and that some of the village houses would be, and in fact still are, in Ennerdale, some, including the parish church, in Kinniside, and others in Kelton, (now merged with Lamplugh.) It must have caused considerable bitterness and rivalry when the lord of one manor charged less rent than his neighbours, and even today some of the older Ennerdale village residents rather grudgingly refer to Kinniside or Lamplugh as 'tuther side'.

Certain customs to ensure the efficient running of the community were built up and included the Court Leet when, once a year, with great pomp and ceremony, the Steward of the Manor and Forest proclaimed an oath of allegiance to the King and the Lord of the Manor and appointed jurors and officials. In 1778, the Steward of the Manor was John Wordsworth of Cockermouth, the father of the poet William Wordsworth. In his capacity as agent for the Lord of the Manor, Sir James Lowther, he swore in:-

James Williamson - Moorend
Thomas Jackson - Laverick Hall
William Jenkinson - Townhead
Henry Bragg
John Lamb
Clement Mossop
John Mossop
John Rogers - Gardenor
John Stainton - Routen
Joseph Bowman
William Rawling
Jonathan Atkinson

William Jenkinson was appointed Grave
James Williamson and John Stainton were appointed Constables
Thomas Jackson and John Stainton were appointed Hedge Lookers

Having got the official bit over, they then got down to serious business in the pub and afterwards presented their account:-

	£	s	d
To Eating	0	13	04
To Ales	0	01	08
To Punch	0	02	00
To Horses	0	01	02
	0	18	02

Records show that the inhabitants were a quarrelsome lot in the 16th and 17th centuries and were forever being fined for misdemeanours like:-

Thomas Benson for drawing blood upon Willyam Birkmoss
Willyam Birkmoss for a Contact made upon Thomas Benson
Richard Birkmosse for hounding the goods of Thomas Benson
Thomas Benson for Listening under the windowe when the Jure were giveinge their verdict
Margareta Patrickson for undecent words
William Wilson for a boxe on the Eare given to his wife
James Williamson for sclanderinge William Jackson for calling him Mare Steeler
Henry Jackson for allowing his daughter to bear a bastard child in his house
John Fisher for unlawful games in his house on the Sabbath day

Village Shop - Cheeney Row - Old Reading Room - Shepherds Arms

According to old records there were three mills in Ennerdale. In 1610 the King granted to Edward Ferrers and Francis Philipps:-

> *all that watermill in Ennerdale, now or late in the tenure of James Milner; and all that watermill in Ennerdale, now or late in the tenure of Anthony Patrickson; and all that fulling mill in Ennerdale*

James Williamson held the first mill, together with six acres called Moorend, in 1560 and his son Nicholas rented the farms of Middle Moorend and Low Moorend. Although the names have changed slightly, these places can still be identified and it suggests that James Williamson's mill was nearby and, in that case, it would very probably have been the ruined mill near the lake marked on maps as 'Ennerdale Mill'. But where the mill operated by Anthony Patrickson, and the fulling mill were located is a complete mystery. Since all mills would be powered by water, it is possible that the fulling mill was at Bleach Green, close to where the river Ehen flows out of the lake, and perhaps on the place where a bleach works was built in 1866. It was owned by the Ainsworth family, who had a spinning mill at Cleator where they manufactured sewing thread and brought hanks of thread to their works at Ennerdale to be bleached. Hence the name Bleach Green. The bleach works was pulled down in the early part of this century and a water treatment works was built in its place. On completion of the new treatment works in 1995, the old works was knocked down and with it another landmark familiar to residents and regular visitors, the old gauge house, which contained equipment used to record the volume of water extracted from the lake. The site is now a car park.

For generations the Ennerdale valley and the village relied heavily on agriculture but, as slate quarrying expanded and significant deposits of iron ore were discovered in the fells around Ennerdale, scores of farm workers abandoned the drudgery of rustic life for the regular hours and relatively high wages offered by the quarry and mine owners. Having lost many of their workers, local farmers must have invented new words to describe the mining companies, but there is no doubt that mining was a tremendous boost to the economy of the area, and in 1871 the population of Ennerdale had shot up to an all-time record of almost 700. It was a

To Be Sold in Public Sale

That old established Paper Mill with a glazing mill in the manufactory and a Dwelling House adjoining situated on BROADMOOR upon the River Ehen, in ENNERDALE with the Mill Wheels and Machinery thereto belonging. The Wheels are nearly new, all utensils and machinery in the best Order for immediate work, and the Situation remarkably good for the Manufacture of White Paper, as the Water which flows from Ennerdale Lake is very pure. Should the Paper Mill not be sold the same will be LET, at the Time above mentioned, to any Person inclined to take the Mill and Machinery on reasonable Terms - Possession is to be given at Whitsuntide next. Also a QUANTITY OF PAPER of various Kinds made at the said Mill, and which will be offered in Lots suitable to Tradesmen. A Deposit of £10 per Cent. is to be paid, and the Remainder of the Purchase money at the End of Three Months. The Mill may be viewed and further particulars known at the office of Mr Hodgson, Solicitor, Whitehaven.

The Cumberland Paquet 24 Feb 1823

Ennerdale Reading Room

On Saturday evening last the Committee of Management of this Institute gave a concert which was well patronised by the public. Mr J.M. Finlinson of Waterloo Villa, Arlecdon was in the Chair. The only drawback to the complete success of the concert was the lateness of arrival of some of the performers and some who never turned up at all. The time for commencing having to be exceeded by half an hour and the audience becoming somewhat impatient, the Chairman ascended the platform and apologised for the detention, expressed his pleasure at being present to assist in the evening's entertainment on behalf of the Reading Room at Ennerdale which he said had now been established a little over ten years. He concluded that tea would be provided at the end of the entertainment after which he introduced the following programme, which considering that many of the performers were volunteers in the place of absentees was very creditably rendered. Mr Webb sang "True until Death". Mr J. McGannen sang "Little Sister's Gone to Sleep". The Chairman sang "Johnny with our Rose".

Whitehaven News Sept 1887.

......and a good time was had by all !

boom period for the building trade, and blank spaces on the village map were soon filled with new buildings, which included Post Office Row, the vicarage, the school, and, just outside the village, the row of cottages at Braemar . The original narrow road winding past the church was by-passed by the 'new road', and a footbridge was built over Croasdale Beck at Tom Butt for the benefit of the miners who walked from the village to the mines at Kelton and Knock Murton.

The new prosperity had its down-side though. With the two pubs bulging with miners on pay day, there were times when the village resembled a scene from the wild west. When the hunts came round the district to spend a week hunting the fells, the whole village joined them on the fells and hardly a miner or a quarryman turned up for work. Inevitably the heavy drinking sessions indulged in by the miners and quarrymen led to violent incidents and, on one occasion, a clerk taking the men's wages from Ennerdale village to the iron ore mine at Knock Murton was attacked and killed and the wages stolen. In the primitive working conditions of an industry that employed young children, there were numerous tragic accidents. On the burial certificate of 11 year old James Francis, of Cleator, who died as a result of an accident in Kinniside lead mine in 1822, the Minister wrote, *'This was an engaging and promising boy. He came to Cleator with his parents and entered upon his employment of attending the crushing mill on the lead mine at Kinnyside wrought by Mr Knott & Co. on Wednesday the 20th of May; and on Friday 30th his left leg and thigh were drawn into the rowlers and shattered to pieces. The thigh was amputated on the Saturday, and he expired during the operation.'*

By the end of the 19th century the prosperity bubble had burst and, with a fall in the demand for iron ore, mining steadily declined and many local men left to seek work in the mines of South Africa. Knock Murton mine managed to continue into the new century until it was abandoned in 1923 and mining in the Ennerdale district ceased for all time.

Though it had nothing like the impact of the mining industry on the local economy, the acquisition of the upper Ennerdale valley by the Forestry Commission in 1925 brought a measure of stability to the area through the creation of jobs for men displaced by the decline of mining. In the course of time the Forestry Commission located an office and store in the village, and houses were built for workers and the foresters, all of which helped to secure the future of the school and stabilise the economy. The building of the nuclear power station at Calder Hall, six miles away, in the 1950s, and the establishment of a nuclear reprocessing plant on the site, brought unprecedented prosperity to West Cumberland which led to a building boom in the village and an increase in the population. Figures for 1997 show the population of Ennerdale village and the Ennerdale valley to be about 96 men and 79 women.

Regrettably, as happened to the mining industry, the influence of the Forestry Commission in Ennerdale village eventually declined and withered. The Commission's commitment to provide employment and housing in rural areas was dropped, and in the late 1980s they closed their office and, together with the forester's and forestry workers' houses, it was offered for sale. In 1997 the majority of the workers were made redundant, and Ennerdale forest is now controlled from the Commission's office near Keswick.

In the early 1900s the Ennerdale and Kinniside Horticultural Society was formed with the intention of holding an annual flower show, but also with the idea of providing an annual treat for the children of the parish. The flower show was eventually extended to include an agricultural section and 'Ennerdale Show', held on the field now occupied by the new houses opposite Vicarage Lane, was a grand affair with a brass band marching through the village and with the road filled with animals being walked to the show. Since those days the show has been held at a variety of locations and the emphasis is now on agriculture, particularly the showing of Herdwick sheep. The show continues to thrive and is now held at the Leapes, a field on the hill above Croasdale, on the last Wednesday in August..

Ennerdale is famous for a strange occurrence which took place in the 19th century and about which countless legends still linger on. In May 1810 farmers were alarmed by the number of sheep they were finding dead and partly eaten on the fells. At times, as many as five or six sheep would be killed in one night, and the situation became so serious parties of shepherds and local workers armed with guns were organised to watch over the sheep, but the killing continued. In an era when country folk were particularly superstitious, rumours circulated that it was the work of the 'Evil One' and there was almost widespread panic in the valley until the culprit was caught in the act and found to be a huge dog:-

He was smooth haired of a tawny mouse colour, with dark streaks in tiger-fashion over his hide, and appeared to be a cross between a mastiff and a greyhound

He was never heard to growl or bark and he was cunning enough to move from one district to another after a kill. A reward of ten pounds for the dog, dead or alive, was offered by Mr John Russell who owned a large area of land in Ennerdale, and packs of foxhounds flanked by scores of men, armed to the teeth and mounted on everything from cart horses to donkeys, scoured the countryside hoping to run the wild dog to earth. Between May and September it killed over 350 sheep and though, during that time, one farmer had managed to wound it with gunshot, it managed to avoid being caught. Finally, on the 11th of September, it was cornered in Eskat wood near Ennerdale and John Steel, a farmer from Asby, earned immortality by firing the shot that killed "T' Girt Dog of Ennerdale."

a short tour ......

The best place to start a tour of the village is from the school, which is prominently situated on an 'island' surrounded by roads. It is not clear when the first school was built on this site. The O.S. map of 1863 shows the school where it is now, but some elderly local people insist that their parents attended school in a schoolroom at Braemar Cottages, half a mile or so outside the village, in 1876. A document dated 1873 gives the building of the school as 1872, and it seems to suggest that the schoolroom at Braemar Cottages was a temporary measure because of overcrowding in the village school. This possibility is strengthened by a letter to the Education Department in London from J.S. Ainsworth, one of the school governors, dated 26 July 1875, which states:-

'The Parish have rebuilt and enlarged the old school and an efficient school is now maintained under government inspection. Owing to recent increase of population it ap-

pears it may be necessary to enlarge the building further. The Trustees are anxious to decide on what is their best course for the future, and in order to do so wish to know exactly what can be required from them by the government.'

Though the wheels of bureaucracy turned painfully slowly, permission to extend the school was eventually given and, on the 3rd of March, 1877, the Secretary of the Education Department wrote to Mr Ainsworth:-

'My Lords are glad to learn that arrangements have been made for enlarging the Ennerdale and Kinniside Parish School. I am to request that a plan of the proposed alterations may at once be forwarded for Their Lordships approval.'

The fine granite building you are looking at was completed about 1878 and the entrance door opened on to the road facing the post office. The teacher at the time was George Sterling, who agreed *'to teach and to serve as Schoolmaster of the said school ... for the gross Government Grant earned by the school during the year.'* In other words, the teacher's pay depended on how many pupils attended the school during the year, and entries in the school log such as, "Very stormy this morning, no school,' and, 'No school today, children helping with harvest,' show that both the weather and farming activities must have played havoc with his pay cheque. Entries in the school log reveal there was often friction between the teacher and the chairman of the school managers, usually the vicar. In December 1898 the teacher wrote angrily in his log:-

The Rev. J. Tyson and Mrs Tyson visited school this afternoon, and am sorry to record the fact that the latter considered the master both vulgar and impertinent and he in turn thought Mrs Tyson had not much room to speak. I hereby record the fact that they were both very rude and impertinent, especially the vicar who states: "I will let you see that I'll be master here."

When, in 1881, the school managers decided to appoint a lady teacher to assist the headmaster, they fell foul of Victorian prudery and the Vicar received an irate letter from the Director of Education in London demanding:- *My Lords wish to know whether the Managers have considered the obvious danger to which this kind of arrangement is exposed unless some older woman will be constantly present while the School is being held.*

The Vicar replied:-

> *'We have the utmost confidence in the Master and Assistant Mistress. I have known the former from his childhood and they are both regular communicants of our church...The mistress has her own schoolroom with separate lobby and fire...She receives no lessons from the Master so there is no need for her to go through the great room, nor for him to enter her classroom. It is not merely on account of the expense that we deprecate the appointment of a matron as it would cause not only surprise and amusement but lead to much undesirable innuendo, suspicion and idle gossip.'*

The letter obviously satisfied 'My Lords of the Education Department' that Miss Glasscodine was not in any moral peril and her appointment was approved at a salary of £35 a year.

Not so successful was the Vicar in retaining the services of Martha Bennet of Lane Foot, the part-time sewing mistress. Clearly disgruntled about her pay, she tendered her resignation:-

> *My husband thinks that Ive staid long enough for the wage that Ive been receiving; and when I was first engaged I understood that as the school increased my wages had to increase also but they have not done so, and my friends all say that Ive been very unkindly dealt with.*

One old village resident who was a pupil at the school in the early 1920s recalls that there were well over a hundred pupils and three teachers at the school, and that because the pupils often got soaked through walking to school in rainy weather the headmaster kept a cupboard full of spare clothes for them to change into. Wet clothes were then hung round an iron stove in the middle of the classroom. The school also had a garden where the pupils grew potatoes and other produce for sale to help the school fund.

In the 1980s the number of pupils dropped to an all-time low and the school was threatened with closure but, thanks to a vigorous local campaign, it was saved. There are now 32 pupils on the register and 2 teachers on the staff.

Immediately opposite the school and facing the local shop / post office there is a signpost pointing to Croasdale. This is the site of a stone-breakers yard where a man was employed to break rocks into small pieces for repairing the road. In 1996 the children of the school built a mosaic of tiles on the edge of the pavement by the signpost depicting life in Ennerdale parish. Each tile has been individually crafted and painted by the children and is a true work of art.

Attached to the shop is a row of cottages called Cheeney Row. Apparently Cheeney was a builder who came to live in Ennerdale from the Isle of Man. In days gone by the shop was the focal point of the village, and supplied everything from sewing cotton, paraffin and groceries to feed stuff, tools, and animal medicines for local farmers. The shop and cottages were built during the mining boom, but the Shepherds Arms Hotel close by was built about 1705. It was originally called 'The Dog and Gun'. The village blacksmith had his smithy behind the hotel, and there was also a reading room that boasted a small library of books and a billiard table. But it was very much a 'men only' club; women were not allowed in! Until it was moved to another part of the village there was also a branch of the Co-op in the same row. All these buildings were pulled down long ago. Like so many rural villages that had to be self-sufficient in the days before there was public transport, Ennerdale had a wide range of tradesmen and women. There were blacksmiths, carpenters, shoemakers, tailors, weavers, masons, dressmakers, plumbers, slaters, tanners and a whole host of others who made an adequate living. They have been displaced by progress and are now just a part of history.

Leave the Shepherds Arms and walk past the house called Brookside - the neatly-kept garden used to be the village garage and petrol station - and on past Vicarage Lane to where the road crosses a bridge over Croasdale Beck. This is the bridge, originally just a footbridge, built for the miners who walked each day to the mines near Kirkland, and it also marks the boundary between the parishes of Ennerdale and Lamplugh. A track on the left, immediately over the bridge, leads to Stockhow Farm once owned by the Patricksons, the 'Kings of Ennerdale.' The small house on the right called 'The Byres.' a short distance beyond the bridge, used to be a farm and the row of cottages attached to it, known as Tom Butt, are reputed to be named after the builder, another immigrant from the Isle of Man. The old white house in the trees opposite, called Pasture Gate, was built for a mine manager but, when the mines closed, was for many years the schoolmaster's house.

A short distance beyond Tom Butt cottages, on the road to Kirkland, is the entrance to Hollins Farm, the home of the Rawling family who have farmed in the Ennerdale area for many generations. In 1794 Joshua Rawling wrote a veterinary book for farmers which was very popular and went into three editions. For many years the Rawling family have also been prominent in the organisation of Ennerdale Show. Beyond the entrance to Hollins, along the Kirkland road, is Stowbank, another farm once owned by the Patricksons.

Returning to the school, the modern house facing it, next to the post office, is on the site of the 'clogger's shop' where the standard footwear of the farmfolk was made and repaired. A little way beyond the post office the road curves round to the river Ehen and the bridge from which the village got its name. Bridge End Cottages, the row of cottages close by the bridge, have in their time housed a joiner's shop, the village police station, the post office, a branch of Cleator Moor Co-op and the Westminster bank. If you look over the bridge on the same side as the cottages, you might be able to make out where the ancient ford crossed the river.

One of the most closely guarded secrets of generations of Ennerdale men is the location of the pearl

The Old Smithy - from a painting by Mrs Mary Bird, Ennerdale Bridge

fishing beds in the River Ehen. In the 17th century one of the Ennerdale Patricksons was granted the pearl fishing rights in the Ravenglass Estuary, and it is believed he had some success in the Ehen as well. The fresh water pearls in the river are not considered to be as valuable as those in the ocean but they are still very attractive. A master in the art of fresh water pearl fishing is Joe Bird of Ennerdale Bridge who, over the years, has collected an interesting selection. In an effort to protect the fresh water pearls, English Nature have declared parts of the river a Site of Special Scientific Interest, and fishing for them is now positively discouraged.

Crossing the bridge, you leave Ennerdale parish and enter Kinniside. The wide road ahead is the 'new road' built to avoid the embarrassment of modern heavy trucks becoming wedged in the narrow 'old road'. Over the bridge turn immediately right and follow the 'old road' to the church. The piece of land on the left, gradually being taken up as a burial ground, used to be the school garden where the scholars grew vegetables and sold them to the villagers.

In 1534, William, Abbot of St Mary of York, granted the people of Ennerdale 'the right to bury' on account of the great distance from the mother church at St Bees, *'provided that the inhabitants maintained the Curate, the Chapel, and its ornaments'*. A chapel and burial ground was founded on the site of the present church, and the first curate was Christopher Wood who was appointed in 1543. Over the centuries there was a long succession of clergymen, but the only one born and bred in Ennerdale was Anthony Nicholson, the son of John Nicholson, Curate of Ennerdale in 1690. Anthony was baptised in Ennerdale Church on February the 8th 1688, and succeeded his father in the Curacy of Ennerdale in 1723.

A strange and tragic entry in an old register reveals how, as a result of the parish overseer's lack of compassion and charity, the church got a new set of pews:-

> *This chapel was pewed September 8 1786 by a fine of £40 which was laid upon one Mathew Jackson of Law in the parish of Millom, who villainously broght one Sarah Ashburn into this parish of Ennerdale in order to lay her upon the said parish of Ennerdale.*

The Fox and Hounds Inn and Church Cottages

The above mentioned Matthew Jackson received the sum of £70 for which he agreed to maintain her for life, but the sum being spent, he the said Mathew Jackson with one Richard Cook of Ulpha did bring Sarah Ashburn to William Hail of Far-thwaite, the overseer of this parish and left her. She the above mentioned Sarah Ashburn finding she could find no assistance from William Hail, set forward to go to Calder-bridge, as it was supposed, but unfortunately was starved to Death upon the mountains, her body was found near the Side. The mountain was at that time covered with snow two feet thick. Sarah Ashburn's body lays buried near the School House which was interred February 27th 1785 by me, James Ponsonby, Minister

When King Charles 11 was persuaded to help the beleaguered wool trade by passing an Act in 1667 ordering that no material should be used in the burial of a body except wool, it seems that the farmers of Ennerdale were not enthusiastic about going to their grave in the knowledge they were helping their neighbour, for no entries appear in the burial registers confirming that an Ennerdale resident was 'buried in woollen.' It wasn't until after the Act was made more stringent in 1678, and the possibility of a hefty fine making a hole in the deceased farmer's legacy, that families began to take the law seriously, and leading Ennerdale farming families are well represented in the burial register of 1681:-

Henry Litledale of Bridge was buried ye 4th day of May
John Scott of Gilliewhait was buried the 4th day of July
John Tyson of Banklands was buried the 17th day of July
All those above-written were buried in wolen

Having survived for three hundred years, the old church was in a poor condition and, on the 14th of March 1856 , the Vicar, William Dukes, invited the rate-payers of Ennerdale and Kinniside to a meeting at the school to discuss what should be done. It was unanimously decided that *'it is desirable that the chapel of Ennerdale be rebuilt and not repaired'*, and a committee of local worthies was appointed to raise funds. The Church Building

St. Mary's Church

Society gave a grant of £60, Charles Eaglesfield, a Maryport architect, was commissioned to design a new building and, before the Bishop of Carlisle could find an argument in favour of retaining the old building, the Vicar quickly petitioned him for a *'Licence for Performance of Divine Service in the Parochial School room at Ennerdale aforesaid during the taking down and rebuilding of the said Chapel.'*

The building of the new church went ahead, and on the 29th of January 1858 William Malone Dukes, *'perpetual Curate of the Chapelry of Ennerdale in the County of Cumberland and Diocese of Carlisle'* informed the Bishop that *'the Chapel of Ennerdale aforesaid hath been taken down and a new one erected in lieu..the said Chapelry is now ready for use and it would be a great convenience to the inhabitants of the said Chapelry if he would be pleased to authorize the performance of Divine Service therein until the same can be duly consecrated.'* The Bishop gave permission for the church to be used, but decided that having an icy wind whistling around his cassock in Ennerdale in January was not for him and postponed the consecration ceremony until the 29th of June 1858, when it was recorded that the *'Honourable and Right Reverend Henry Montagu Villiers Lord Bishop of Carlisle consecrated the Church of Ennerdale.'*

For centuries the Vicar's salary depended on the income from tithes, a payment extracted annually from the parishioners, and on the rent from glebe land owned by the church. Ennerdale church seems to have been particularly well off for glebe land, owning Whins Farm, near the lake, and land at Keswick and Egremont, though for some reason not explained in church records, one of the fields at Whins farm was owned by Buttermere Chapel. To cash in on the iron ore mining boom, the incumbent in 1902 leased the mineral rights of the land at Egremont to the Wyndham Mining Company, but twenty years later mining was in the doldrums and a letter to William Jardine, the Vicar in 1924, warned, *'The flooding of the mine has brought to an end all prospect of any more income from that source - i.e. from the iron ore.'*

The church is well worth a visit, and inside you'll find more information about its history, including the association with the poet William Wordsworth who wrote his poem 'The Brothers' after visiting Ennerdale in 1799. The church bell is said to have come from a monastery at St Bees which was destroyed in the reign of

Henry V111, and is thought to be at least 700 years old.

Immediately opposite the church gate is the 'Fox and Hounds' Inn, but to reach it you have to cross the village's third bridge, Monk's Bridge, which spans Rowland Beck. There would have been a ford here at one time, but the flow of water is barely a trickle compared to the unpredictable river Ehen. The 'Fox and Hounds' is probably one of the oldest buildings in the village and has had several different names. In 1765 it was the 'Bridge Inn,' in 1794 the 'White Bear,' and in 1863 the 'Hare and Hounds.'

The nearby row of cottages, appropriately known as 'Church Cottages,' is very old and the last two cottages on the right in the row are on the spot of the first Vicarage. John Nicholson and his wife Elinor lived there in 1690 and their son Anthony, who succeeded his father as Vicar, was probably born in the house. In the early 1900s a lady who lived in the middle of the row sold home-made gingerbread and treacle toffee.

Walking between the Fox and Hounds and Church Cottages you pass the row of modern houses built for the forestry workers, before emerging onto the 'new road' by a house built on the site of the Forestry Commission's office. The fine house immediately opposite is Scaur Head. Also known as the Parsonage, for many years it replaced the cottages by the church as the Vicar's residence until William Jukes, the incumbent in 1858, persuaded the Bishop to build a larger Vicarage, on the right higher up the hill beyond Scaur Head. In 1992 this Vicarage was deemed uneconomical to maintain and was sold. A new Vicarage was built on the smart housing estate in Vicarage Lane.

Just past the old Vicarage is the road that goes over Cold Fell to Calder Bridge. A short distance along the road on the left is a dwelling called Lane Foot, the home of John Ray, cobbler and shoe-maker, in 1851, and who was the sexton of Ennerdale church for forty seven years. Across the fields to the right behind Lane Foot, tucked in the shelter of the fellside, is Fell End Farm. In 1843 it was owned by an eccentric character called Willy Lamb, who disliked spending money on repairing the property and, when it rained, the only dry spot in the house where his family could find shelter was under a large oak beam across the open fireplace!

I don't want to take you too far away from the village, but if you walk a little further up the Cold Fell road you will see Swinside Farm perched on the fellside on your right, and there is such a lovely story about how it got its name I thought it worth including. About the year 1320 Lord Egremont organised a deer hunt to celebrate the marriage of his daughter Margaret to Lord Lucie, and a large cavalcade of riders rode out of Egremont Castle heading for Copeland Forest. In the excitement of the chase, Lord Lucie and his bride were separated from the party and stumbled on a wild boar that charged Lucie's horse and killed it. Lord Lucie was thrown to the ground and knocked unconscious. Margaret's pony swerved in terror and she was flung off. The boar was charging towards her when the sound of a hunting horn distracted it, and in a second it was dead with a spear in its side. Guided by the sound of the horn, Lord Egremont and his party reached the scene to find Lord Lucie and Margaret lying unconscious, and close by three wild boar, killed by the hunter called Towerson. Overcome with gratitude, Lord Egremont turned to him and said:-

A hyde of land
Son of de Tours, thine hence shall be
For this brave act of fealty
And the memory of this day
In Copeland ne'er shall fade away
And to recall the wild brawn's lair
The name of Swineshyde it shall bear.

Return to the school for a tour of the valley and forest.

the valley ......

Leaving the school, follow the road signposted to Croasdale. It passes High Bridge Farm on the right and then, on a bend, the curiously named Lillyhall, a neat little cottage with a rather grand name. Continue on past the entrance to Low Moor End farm to a road junction, and turn down the road where the signpost points to Ennerdale Lake - even the local authority has got the name wrong! On the right is Braemar Cottages, now converted into two smart houses but at one time it was a row of four cottages. The end one on the right housed the village school in 1876 and later was a pub called the Mechanics Arms. On the left is Broadmoor Plantation, owned by the Forestry Commission. Beyond Braemar and the entrance to Far Moor End farm, the road swings left while a track turns off to the right by a large modern house. In the days when the Ainsworth family of Cleator owned much of the land on this side of the lake, at the turn of the century, there were three cottages here, one of which was occupied by the Ainsworths' gamekeeper. A public footpath runs past the house and goes by Ennerdale Mill to Crag Fell, but the ruined mill is on private property, so please keep out. There has been a mill on this spot since the 16th century and probably earlier; and though for many centuries it was most likely a corn mill grinding flour for local farmers, it was shown on the map as a paper mill in 1774. It was still a paper mill well into the next century but, in 1824 the tenant, Jonathan Head, went bust and was forced to sell up - see page 33. The mill was given a new lease of life as a corn mill again but, like so many rural mills driven by water power, advancing technology made it uneconomical and eventually it went out of business. For some time the building was converted to a saw mill where trees from the estate were converted into planks and boards, but eventually that ceased and the mill is now in ruins.

Continuing along the road to a sharp right hand bend, you'll see a lane going straight ahead into the forest. This is Sawdust Lonning, and it got its name during the 1914-18 war when Broadmoor Wood was being felled for the war effort. Three large portable sawmills driven by steam traction engines sawed up the logs, and when the sawdust piled up and clogged the saws, the traction engines pulled the sawmills a few metres along the track. In time, the sawmills left behind a covering of sawdust several feet deep the whole length of the lonning (lane). Sawdust Lonning is the old access road to the site of the now demolished Anglers Inn, and a public right of way.

Having followed the road round the bend you'll come to a Forestry Commission car park and the entrance to a camp site owned by the Scout Association, but continue on over the bridge ahead to a car park on the left. This is Bleach Green, and the car park is on the site of the old bleach works. The nearby cottages were occupied by the works manager and his assistant. The low dam on the edge of the lake was originally built by Ainsworths, the owners of the water-powered bleach works, to ensure a constant flow to the water wheels, but in more recent times it has been raised by the water authorities who use the lake as a supply of drinking water.

the lake ......

Sometimes called Broadwater in old documents - in 1626 Joseph Patrickson paid fourpence *'for the fishing of Broadwater and the 'Little Isle'* - Ennerdale Water, or Ennerdale Lake as it is popularly known, is the remotest and least known of the region's lakes but it has inspired poets and captivated romantics for centuries. Overcome by its beauty a visitor in 1795 wrote:-

> *It forms a picture, such as the canvas never presented; it embraces a variety, so distributed, as no pencil can ever imitate. No designer in romance ever alloted such a residence to his fairy inhabitants*

The building of the dam by Ainsworths for their bleach works in 1866, and the raising of the level by water authorities at various times, has extended the area of the lake quite considerably since ancient times. In 1997 it was a touch over 2.50 miles long (4 Km) by 0.75 miles (1Km) wide, with the deepest point about 150 feet

(45 mtrs) close to the east side of Anglers Crag. Fed by the River Liza and numerous mountain becks, the lake is reputed to have some of the purest water in the country. Years ago it was well stocked with fish. Eels, sea trout and salmon used to be caught in the River Liza upstream beyond Gillerthwaite, but the ravages of time have taken their toll and the fish are not as prolific as they were.

The lake is the home of the mysterious char, a fish similar to the brown trout but:-

> *About eight ounces...most splendidly coloured, red and gold bellied, fins with a pink shade in the centre, shaded into a brown ash blue and edged with pearl colour...a most brilliant and elegant creature*

The Char lives in deep water in the lake and at one time was considered a great delicacy. Acknowledging delivery of potted char sent from the Lake District to his London home in 1738, Lord Montagu wrote:-

> *I received the Pott of Charr which you sent by that day's Carrier, which was the best I ever eat, and I would have you send me some of the same sort by every Carryer, take care to Pick the hen fish and those that are of the Red Kind, and let them be potted and seasoned just as that Pot was, for it cant be beter*

On February 23, 1666, Sir Daniel Fleming of Rydal, near Ambleside, paid, *'John Bankes, 9s.0d, for the Carryage of a char-pye unto the Earl of Carlisle at London, being 4 stone and 5 lb'*. The Earl must have feasted well on a pie that weighed 28 kilos! Some early travellers in the Lake District called the fish, 'Red Charre', 'Gilt Charre' or the 'Char-fish', but the historian Denton, who was always flamboyant with his descriptions, called it the 'Golden Alpine Trout'. Char are found in several lakes in the Lake District and have different breeding habits, but every year, in November, the Ennerdale Char surface after dark in their hundreds and make for Smithy Beck and the mouth of the Liza to lay their eggs in the gravel beds. In the 1930s it was discovered that the lake was the only place in Britain where a minute freshwater crayfish with the impressive latin name of

Limnocalanus Macrurus was known to exist. It caused a stir of excitement in the scientific world and led to speculation that the lake was once connected with the sea. Since the surface of the lake is 368ft (113 mtrs) above sea level, it is a phenomenon geologists have argued over for years. Meantime the little beastie has not been recorded in any survey since 1956, and is now believed to be extinct in this country.

The small island, now barely visible following several increases in the level of the lake this century, is called The Little Isle, and is in fact a smooth-sided pinnacle 150 feet high (45mtrs) which, it is said, would be more difficult to climb than Pillar Rock if the lake ever dried out. The pinnacle would certainly be an impressive land mark!

For very many years the lake was part of the estate of the Dickinson family of Red How, Lamplugh, and jealously protected. When, in October 1848, John Tyson, a local farmer, was caught tipping stones into the lake he was made to write an apology to the Dickinsons and pay a fine of sixpence (2.5p) for trespassing. Joseph Dickinson was furious when, in 1849, the Trustees of Whitehaven Town and Harbour having found *'Water for the use of this said Town and Neighbourhood and of the Shipping resort of the said Port and Harbour totally inadequate and insufficient for that purpose'*, obtained an Act of Parliament to lay a pipe from the river Ehen just below the lake and build a weir to raise the level of the lake by one foot. Antagonism between the parties smouldered on for nearly thirty years, then in 1873 burst into a full scale row when Joseph Dickinson discovered that the Whitehaven Trustees had been quietly selling water to the Parish of Moor Row. He wrote to the Trustees angrily complaining that this was outside the terms of the Act, but he would give his consent in return for half the net profits from the new supply. Smugly confident that they had Parliament on their side, the Trustees replied that they were quite unable to accede to his demand, and awaited his orders to turn off the supply to the inhabitants of Moor Row. This bureaucratic blackmail sparked off a flurry of correspondence between Dickinson and his lawyers, and they had interminable meetings with the Whitehaven Trustees; but months went by and they were no nearer reaching an agreement. Finally someone suggested, quite unheard of in an era of complete male domination, that a woman's opinion should be sought. There must have been a lot of disgruntled mutterings behind the assembled Victorian beards, but it was agreed that

Joseph's wife should be consulted. With typical female astuteness, she went straight to the point. "Do the people of Moor Row need the water?' she asked. "Yes," replied her husband. "Then they shall have it," said his wife calmly; and that was the end of the matter.

Some time later, obviously taking advantage of having an unwitting ally in Mrs Dickinson, the Whitehaven Trustees sent a telegram to Joseph Dickinson that read, *'Please give permission for a supply of water to Cleator Moor. Complete famine and likelihood of disease. Are afraid of riots.'* Joseph didn't bother to consult his wife. He replied giving his permission!

After successfully winning the right in 1885 to extract water from Ennerdale, the Whitehaven Authority presented another Bill to Parliament in 1899 which would give them further power to raise the level of the lake. The Whitehaven Corporation Bill was vigorously contested by the Dickinsons, but a letter from their London lawyers, dated 2nd August 1899, which stated briefly, *'This Bill received the Royal Assent yesterday,'* gave the depressing news that they had lost the case. Permission was given to raise the level of the lake by one foot (30 centimetres) but it is believed that the permitted rise was ignored and, in fact, the level was raised considerably more. The official published figures showed a rise in the level of the lake between 1848 and 1946 of three feet six inches, (1.06 mtrs,) but knowledgeable people who compared landmarks on the shoreline claimed that the actual rise was in fact nearer to seven feet.

In the 1940s, Whitehaven Corporation claimed they needed more water in order to attract new industry to West Cumbria, and announced their intention to raise the level of the lake by a further five feet. It caused an uproar; particularly when it was revealed that Ennerdale's most renowned landmark, the Anglers Inn, built on the lake shore, would be submerged and a large expanse of farm land flooded, and a Public Inquiry was opened in Whitehaven on the 6th of October 1946. During the proceedings, a water engineer engaged by Whitehaven Corporation gave an assurance that, if it was decided that a hotel was essential as an amenity, the Corporation would replace it with another; but, he added, they did not want to, because the effluent from the Anglers went into the lake. Mr Ronald Dickinson, who had taken over the management of Red

How estate, which still owned the lake and the Anglers Inn, said that if the Corporation was prepared to give an undertaking that a similar hotel would be provided in reasonable time he was prepared to withdraw his objection to the scheme, and that he was prepared to provide the land, access to the hotel, and even the water supply. A solicitor for the tenant of the Anglers made a similar offer to withdraw. A lot of hard talking went on behind the scenes, and then the tremendous announcement was made that an agreement had been reached between the parties and that Ronald Dickinson and his tenant had withdrawn their objections to the lake being raised. Being the forthright man he was, Ronald Dickinson would never have agreed to withdraw his objections to the scheme had he not received a concrete assurance from the Corporation that the Anglers would be rebuilt; but when, in December 1946, Whitehaven's Town Clerk announced that the Minister of Health had given the 'go-ahead' for the level of the lake to be raised, he made no mention of the Anglers or of an agreement to rebuild it. Perhaps Ronald Dickinson reminded him of the Corporation's promise, for when, in May 1947, a local angling club applied for the fishing rights on the lake they were informed that:-

> *'The Corporation have decided in conformity with an undertaking given to Mr R. Dickinson to offer fishing rights to the tenant of the new Anglers Inn'*

It was a clear sign that the rebuilding of the Anglers was very much on the Corporation's agenda but, while work to increase the height of the dam was going ahead, a major company who had planned to re-locate to West Cumberland decided to go elsewhere and the Ennerdale scheme was revised and plans for a new Anglers Inn scrapped. Probably, by now, heartily sick of Whitehaven Corporation and their water scheme, Ronald Dickinson appears to have indicated his readiness to negotiate the transfer of ownership of the Anglers Inn and, in March 1949, the Minister of Health informed Whitehaven Corporation that he was prepared to issue a loan for its purchase:-

> *Subject to an assurance by the Corporation that adequate sewage work will be carried out to prevent pollution of the lake by effluent from the hotel; that the hotel will not be demolished or displaced and that it will not be converted into a lido or pleasure ground.*

The Anglers Inn was acquired by the Corporation and in the fullness of time by the South Cumberland Water Board.

the valley again ......

Before going to look at the Anglers Inn site, just walk along the track past the cottages towards the white farmhouse below the fell. In the early part of this century Crag Farm was used as a hunting lodge by the Ainsworth family, but it's not the farm I want to show you. If you look to the right, behind the cottages, you will see what appears to be a collection of attractive stone and slate farm buildings. In the past, when the level of the lake dropped very low during the summer, mobile pumps had to be brought to maintain a flow of water into the river Ehen. During 1992 to 1995, to overcome the problem, the water authority installed a pipe running from a deep part of the lake to a control system on land, and very sensitively designed buildings to house it that would blend with the landscape.

Returning to Braemar cottages, turn right at the road junction, follow the road to the next junction, and turn right again. The farm ahead is How Hall (or Carswell How) one time home of the infamous 'Kings of Ennerdale,' the Patricksons. You are not allowed to enter the farm; but just past the house, on the gable end of the barn, there is a sandstone plaque let into the wall with the inscription *'This house was built A.D. 1566 by Anthony Patrickson and Frances his wife, daughter of Sir Thomas Swinburne, one of the Privy Council to King Henry V111.'*

Continue down the lane to the edge of the lake and the National Trust's parking area, where a solitary weathered sandstone gate post and ruined jetty is all that remains of the old Anglers Inn, or the Boathouse as it was known to local people. Some writers claim that there was an inn on this site in Elizabethan times, but I have never come across any document which mentions it, nor is it marked on very early maps. An 1847 guide to Cumberland devotes a few lines to Ennerdale Water and states, *'Joseph Dickinson built a comfortable inn a few years ago where boats are kept for the accommodation of anglers.'* Joseph Dickinson could not have chosen a more idyllic site for his inn, and for well over a century the whitewashed building set by the edge of the lake was a well known landmark and the jewel of Ennerdale.

A Memorandum of Agreement, dated 11th of March 1850, between James Buchanan, the tenant of the Anglers Inn and William Russill of Langriggreen states that:-

> *William Russill agrees to give and James Buchanan agrees to take the sum of 2/6d per day for the Hire of his Boate for the Rafting of Wood from the Side Wood to the foot of Ennerdale Lake.*

It seems that the lake was a useful highway for transporting wood and stone and when, in 1880, John Weeks and his son Sennet Weeks were granted the tenancy of

> *'all that tenement or dwelling house known by the sign of the 'Anglers Inn'...and also the lake or piece of Water known by the name of Ennerdale Lake...and liberty of boating or fishing on the said Lake..*

it was written into the lease that they also had the sole right of:-

> *placing Boats, Rafts or Steamers thereon for the purpose of carrying and conveying up, down, over and upon the said Lake, Wood, Stone, Minerals or other Materials and taking a toll for the same.'*

By 1899 the Weeks family had moved on, and in June of that year Mr Halifax, the new tenant, wrote an angry letter to Joseph Dickinson complaining that so much damage had been done to his boats by a party of children he would not be able to pay his rent.. He enclosed a newspaper cutting that gave an account of the Egremont Methodist Sunday School's outing to How Hall, Ennerdale:-

> *whither the teachers, scholars and friends, to the number of almost 200, drove in seven wagonettes....After tea a variety of pleasurable amusements were pursued with vigour.*

Acording to Mr Halifax, the 'pleasurable amusements' included swarming all over his boats and he wrote in his letter, *'I cannot say on paper all I would wish.'*

The access road to the Inn from Ennerdale Bridge was by Sawdust Lonning and along the edge of the lake, and although in 1838 Joseph Dickinson employed William Frears to build a road between How Hall and the Inn, he refused to allow it to be used as a public highway. For farmers living on the north side of the lake it was a handy short cut to the village but, determined to make his point, Joseph must have caught three of them heading along his road. A hastily scribbled document in Joseph's handwriting forces the trio to state that:-

> *'We the undersigned being the owners and/or occupiers of the undermentioned estates situate in the Township of Ennerdale hereby admit that we have no legal right or title to use the private road leading past How Hall to the Anglers Inn and that we have used and still use such road by sufferance only at the pleasure of the owner of the How Hall estate and the Anglers Inn and we herewith pay as an acknowledgement of such admission the sum of one penny each which is so long as we may be respectively allowed to use such road to be paid annually. - September 1888*
>
> *John Bowman, Mireside*
> *William Tyson, Gillerthwaite*
> *John R. Watson, South Mosses*

In 1925, George Dickinson, Joseph's successor, was still insisting that the road was not a public right of way, and placed a notice in the Whitehaven News warning that on Friday the 23rd of October the road would be closed to all vehicular traffic except upon payment of one penny, and he stationed his gamekeepers on guard. Having extracted pennies from 'Mr Curwen, Visitor of Anglers Hotel; Traveller from Whitehaven, Anglo American Oil Company car and Mr Telford, Fruiterer, Frizington', one of the keepers wrote a note reporting *'The only visitors with vehicles were the above - plus the postman who again contended that as a government official he was entitled to go on his bike but eventually he gave way and paid his penny. It was afterwards returned to him as a matter of grace.'*

The location of the Anglers Inn may have been idyllic, but the relationship between the local authority and the Dickinson Estate was anything but. The Dickinson family spent a great deal of money defending the lake from any form of exploitation, but once the local authority gained control of the lake they were powerless. Each time the authority raised the height of the dam, the water advanced ever closer towards the Inn door, and flooding around the Inn was so severe the Sanitary Authority medical officer reported:-

> *a passage from the Boathouse to the farm steadings beyond can only be obtained by passing bodily through the lake for about 60 or 70 yards at a depth of 2 to 4 feet. An open stream, or beck, which flows through the background of the Boathouse is polluted by infiltration from a large middenstead and privy.'*

With the lake impounded for use as public drinking water, the disposal of sewage was a serious problem at the Anglers and it attracted the attention of John Smith, Inspector of Nuisances for Whitehaven Rural District Council, who, on the 1st of August 1901, served Mrs Halifax, who had succeeded to the tenancy following the death of her husband, with a warning that:-

> *I being satisfied of the existance of a Nuisance...arising from sewage flowing into the lake in a crude state do hereby require you...to clean out the cesspool and continue to do so at least once a month.*

Perhaps balking at the prospect of emptying the cesspit with a shovel and wheelbarrow every month,

Mrs Halifax gave notice that she was giving up the Anglers and the tenancy was taken over by William Mulley. He seems to have come to terms with the archaic plumbing until, some time later, he casually mentioned to George Dickinson that he had found a broken pipe under the floor and for months the waste had been flowing under the sitting room instead of into the sewer, *'which would account for the awful smell we had last summer'*. The estate hastened to get a new system installed, which included 'a new lavatory with iron cistern and mahogany seat (no flap), price £5-10s.'

In 1905 the foundations of the Inn and the road along the shore were being eroded so seriously by flooding, the Water Authority was obliged to build a retaining wall, extending from some distance south of the Anglers almost to Bowness Knott. With boats for hire and plenty of fish in the lake, the Anglers Inn was a fisherman's paradise, but it was a great favourite with the locals as well. Every year, a sports meeting was held there with wrestling bouts, running races, obstacle races, sack races, a fell race, singing , hallooing, horn blowing contests, and all the other events, including a hound trail, that made up a typical Cumberland sports day. At certain times of the year it was a popular venue for sheep sales, when farmers from all over the district drove their surplus Herdwicks down from the fells into pens erected for the day by the edge of the lake.

The reputation of Ennerdale's 'Anglers Inn' was legendary and it was as much a part of the landscape as the fells; but, at four o clock on the afternoon of Tuesday the 26th of March 1911, disaster struck. Fire broke out in an attic and smoke was seen pouring from under the roof. William Mulley and his staff rushed upstairs to try and put it out, but there was a strong wind blowing that fanned the flames and within minutes the upper part of the building was ablaze. A messenger was dispatched on a bike to raise Cleator Moor Fire Brigade, six miles away, and in the meantime neighbouring farmers, who had seen the smoke and hurried to help, formed a bucket chain from the lake while others helped to drag furniture outside. The firefighters had to run for their lives when, with a tremendous roar and mass of sparks, part of the roof fell in and, whipped on by the wind, the flames increased and the heat was almost unbearable. With incredible courage some of the men grabbed saws and axes and, climbing into a part of the roof the flames hadn't reached, cut through the beams;

but though it slowed the spread of the fire, it was clear the building was doomed. At 6-45 p.m., two and three quarter hours after the fire had started, Cleator Moor Fire Brigade's horse-drawn fire engine swept into the yard with a clatter of hooves and a loud ringing of bells, but try as they might, the crew could not get the hand-operated pump to work and, by the time the first jet of water squirted out of it, the fire had been brought under control by the old-fashioned bucket chain passed from hand to hand from the lake to the fire. After the last flame had been dowsed, all that was left standing were the walls, the kitchen, the cellar and a couple of rooms above them. The cause of the blaze was never identified, but it was thought that roof beams built into the chimney may have caught fire.

A year or so after the fire, a larger and attractively designed new inn was built close to the old site, but the Anglers was the constant target of officialdom which appeared dedicated to finding a reason for declaring it a health hazard and having it removed. In the 1960s the building was in need of renovation, and though the tenant offered to put his own money in if the water authority would also assist financially and give him a seven year lease, the request was denied. The Water Authority announced they were planning a major scheme which would raise the level of the lake very considerably, and it would submerge the Anglers Inn. At a meeting in Whitehaven on the 1st of October 1968, the South Cumberland Water Board decided that the Anglers should be demolished. An observer at the time wrote:-

> *The new scheme will affect the lake more drastically than ever before. We may sincerely hope that...the Water Board will honour the undertaking given by the Whitehaven Corporation at the Public Inquiry of 1946 and written into the scheme as a condition of the approval, that a new hotel should be built of the same type - that is small, comfortable and residential, and not a weekend drinking resort,which may continue to serve the convenience of anglers and visitors.*

Shortly afterwards the bulldozers reduced one of the gems of the Lake District to a heap of rubble. The scheme to further raise the level of the lake never went ahead, nor was the undertaking to rebuild the Anglers Inn ever honoured.

The Original Anglers Inn

Leaving the site of the Anglers Inn, go back up the lane by How Hall farm and, turning right at the road junction, follow the road as it twists and turns in the direction of Croasdale. A short distance along the road a narrow lane turns off to the right marked with an 'Unfit for Motors' sign. This leads to Howside Farm and Croftfoot Cottage, but ignore it and continue on for Croasdale. As the buildings of Croasdale come into sight, the road sweeps round a sharp left hand bend known locally as 'Stone Heap Corner'. There used to be a stonebreakers yard here where men laboriously prepared 'shillies' (road-mending material).

Croasdale sometimes spelt Crosedale, Crossdale or Crows Dale - is a very ancient hamlet where, at various times, there were three thriving farms, a Methodist chapel, a hat factory, a joiners shop and a tea room. The hat factory closed very many years ago, as did the chapel and the joiners shop. Farming ceased in the late 1970s or early 1980s and, with the exception of one farmhouse which is permanently occupied, all the other dwellings and the old chapel are now holiday homes. Entering Croasdale the road passes a small cottage with the intriguing name of 'Wits End'. According to local people it used to be called 'Lovers Abode' and though I suspect the story of how it came to be called 'Wits End' may well be nothing more than a good Cumberland 'tale', it's worth telling. Apparently the cottage was at one time occupied by the former owner of the Grand Hotel in Whitehaven, who had fallen on hard times when his hotel went on fire and burnt to the ground. He moved to Croasdale at his 'wits end' because he had been forced to give up his life as a hotelier and move to such a remote spot. Why he chose to give the cottage a name that was a constant reminder of his dilemma we will probably never know; but, for what it's worth, that is the story of how it came to be called 'Wits End'.

Mid Town Farm, the house set back on the right beyond Wits End, was once a working farm but for many years, up to the 1960s, it was a tea room called 'The Singing Kettle' run by Miss Daisy Brown. She made delicious home-baked cakes and served tea in real China cups and saucers. There used to be a large kettle, painted red, hung from a post in her garden.

The building on the opposite side of the road - with a telephone box by the gable end - has a fascinating history. It was originally a row of three cottages belonging to Croasdale Farm - just behind the building, hidden in the trees - but John Potter, who bought the farm in 1875, was a deeply religious man and he set aside the middle cottage for use as a chapel for services conducted by the Bible Christians, and later by the Primitive Methodists. When John Potter died in 1899 and Mark, one of his sons, inherited the farm, religious services at the chapel were continued, but when Mark died in 1919 and the farm was sold, the new owners were less than enthusiastic about having a chapel on their doorstep. One Sunday when the congregation turned up for a service they found the chapel door locked and were told that the key had been lost. The same happened the following Sunday, and kept happening until John Potter Jnr, Mark's brother who farmed at Howside - on the 'Unfit for Motors' road - invited the worshippers to hold their meetings in his barn. They were held there until 1921 when John Potter moved to Bank End farm, a mile or so north of Ennerdale Bridge, and at his own expense renovated a disused Bible Mission Chapel at the nearby village of Kirkland. The Kirkland chapel closed in 1994. The old cottages and chapel at Croasdale lay derelict until the building was renovated for use as a holiday home in the late 1970s.

One of the mysteries of Croasdale is the exact location of the Beaver hat factory, which made a range of bowler hats but went out of business shortly before the turn of the 19th century. Mrs Ruth Nevinson of Kirkland, the grand-daughter of John Potter and now an elderly lady, remembers her grandparents talking about the hat makers and thinks the factory was in a building between the three cottages and the farmhouse and was pulled down while she was still a child.

The road swings round sharply to the right by the chapel and the access lane straight ahead is to two farms which have almost identical names. Though there is some evidence that it was originally called Hightown, the farm immediately ahead is known locally only as 'Croasdale,' and the one on the left, 'Croasdale Farm.'

Leaving Croasdale hamlet, the road twists and turns and drops down to Whins Farm, where the 'Unfit for

Motors' road emerges. Whins Farm is very old and at one time was part of the glebe land owned by Ennerdale Church. In 1878 the tenant, Abraham Southward, incurred the wrath of John Wordsworth, the Vicar, to the extent that he received a notice to quit the farm *'on the 25th day of March 1879...and in case of your neglecting or refusing to do so...proceedings will be had against you'.* What sin Abe Southward had committed against the church is not recorded, but he was evicted from Whins and went to live in one of the cottages next to Croasdale chapel. On the fellside above Whins is the ruin of Gill house, once a thriving farm, but the land was merged with Whins long ago and the house fell into ruin. A similar fate befell the little farm of Hollins that nestled in a clump of trees at the foot of Herdus. It is now merged with Mireside Farm, and about twenty years ago most of the stone from the house ruin was removed for repair work at How Hall Farm.

If you have an interest in the history of Lakeland rock climbing, walk the short distance along the 'Unfit for Motors' road to Croftfoot Cottage and pay homage to the memory of John Atkinson, who was born there and was the first man to climb Pillar Rock. See page 88. (You'll have to pay homage from the side of the road; the cottage is on private land.)

Beyond Whins the road narrows and descends to Routen Farm, passing the access track to Beckfoot and Mireside Farm on the way. Both are ancient farmsteads, but now only Mireside is a working farm. There used to be a farm called Banklands adjacent to it but it fell into ruin many years ago. Beckfoot is the base of the National Trust Ranger responsible for the Trust's property in Ennerdale and Loweswater. The National Trust owns or controls a considerable amount of property and land in Ennerdale, including the Anglers Inn site, the farms of Mireside, Howside and How Hall, Side Wood on the south side of the lake, various other bits and pieces by the lake and a large expanse of the fells.

For many years Routen Farm, sometime spelt Roughton, was owned by the Williamson family, whose forebears tenanted Ennerdale Mill in the 16th century and whose descendants still live in Ennerdale. Pet Whins, the name of a field at Routen, was once owned by Buttermere Chapel and the rent from it was part of the Vicar's salary. Up to 1920 the Williamsons ran Routen as a farm and Temperance Hotel, and provided their guests with the luxury of electric light from a home-made hydro electricity plant in Routen Beck. The late Charles Williamson, who died in 1992 at the age of 96, told me that his mother was a great believer in the power of herbal remedies. One of her favourites was Bogweed, which was taken home, boiled, then strained into a jug. "A couple of drinks of that beat all your Epsom Salts for putting you right," said Charlie. A useful cure for blood poisoning was covering the cut with a poultice of cow muck that had been heated on a shovel over the kitchen fire! In the late 1980s Routen was sold and the new owners introduced a unique photographic attraction into the valley when they filled the meadows with Peruvian Llamas.

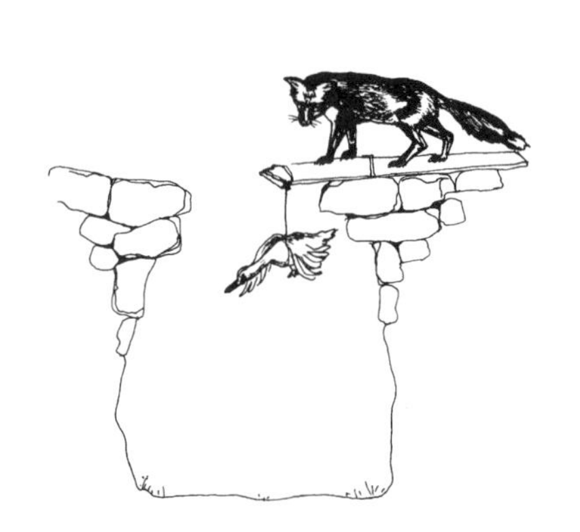

Past Routen, the road traverses along the foot of Herdus and crosses a small bridge over Rake Beck at the edge of the forest. Rake Beck flows down the fell between Herdus and Brown Howe, the little hill to the left of the forest, and if you are fit it is worth climbing the path up Brown Howe to look at the Goose Bield, a circular beehive-shaped stone construction. It was used for trapping foxes in by-gone days when hill farmers eked a meagre living and the loss of lambs to predators could have had a catastrophic effect on a farmer and his family.

Reaching the top of Brown Howe, with Rake Beck on your left follow the rocky path beside the beck as it climbs towards a waterfall. It is quite safe and the bield is soon reached on a little knoll with a superb view over the lake. As the sketches illustrate, a plank of wood was fixed to overhang inside the bield with a goose, or more probably an old hen, hanging on the end of it. When a fox walked along the plank hoping for a feed the plank tipped and the fox fell into the bield. The sides were built to curve inwards and, unable to jump out, the fox was trapped.

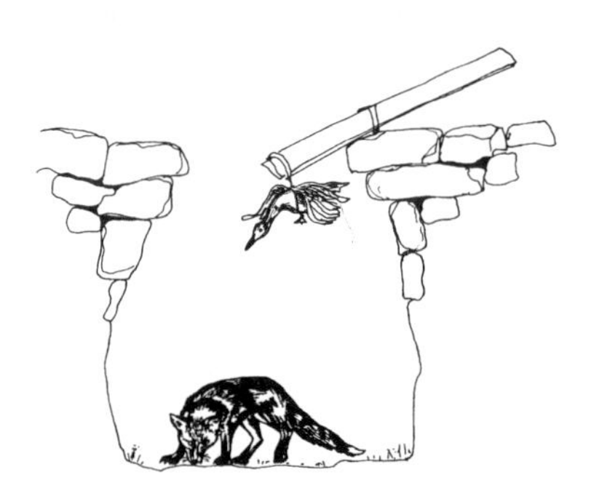

The path above the bield climbs to the summit of Great Borne and, provided you are properly equipped and an experienced walker, it is a very pleasant walk.

Returning down Brown How to the road, continue on below the wooded slopes of Bowness Knott, passing the very ancient Bowness Cottage on the right, to the Forestry Commission's car park and the entrance to the forest, beyond which unauthorised vehicles are not allowed to venture. It is the only valley left in the Lake District from which public access is barred unless you are on foot, on a bike or on a horse, and it is an oasis of peace worth preserving.

Before entering the forest, climb the little hill facing the car park to enjoy the superb view of the lake and Crag Fell and Grike on the opposite shore. At the foot of Crag Fell the crumbling outcrop of Anglers Crag plunges vertically into the water, close to the deepest part of the lake. Why the map makers of the Ordnance Survey call a rocky step on the crag 'Robin Hood's Chair' no-one knows, but if the hero of Sherwood Forest could tear himself away from the lovely Maid Marion to sit gazing into a Cumberland lake it says a lot for the beauty of Ennerdale. Perhaps he came to confer with Gog and Magog, the names of the two prominent pinnacles you can see dominating the skyline above Anglers Crag like petrified giants watching over the valley. Gog and Magog have a relation who stands on the bed of the lake with just the top of his head showing above the water. That's the tiny island you can see in the middle of the lake to the right of Anglers Crag and at over 150 feet (45 metres) from head to toe, he's a real lake giant. He is called the 'Little Isle' in old records, but, since most of the time you can only see the top of his head, perhaps he ought to be called Watergog!

To the left of Anglers Crag is Side Wood, mentioned frequently in ancient documents as being well stocked with deer and a favourite hunting ground of the Lords of the Manor. It is one of the few remaining examples of the Oak forests that once covered the fells and valleys. For centuries Side Wood was pillaged by charcoal burners and ship builders and there is a well-preserved charcoal burner's hut and burning platform in the wood a short distance above the edge of the lake. There is also an old stone jetty on the shore from where charcoal and timber were transported by rafts and boats. On the 6th of October 1949, Lord Lonsdale's Estate sold Side Wood to the National Trust, who have fenced it off to encourage natural regeneration. The 'Round the Lake' footpath passes through Side Wood. and it is an easy and most enjoyable walk.

Turning away from the lake, and standing with your back to it, you look down on the Forestry Commission's car park and across to the scree strewn slopes of Bowness Knott. Peregrine falcons used to nest on the crags and it was fascinating to watch them, but when thieves stole their eggs they moved away. For centuries this was the Parish quarry and the scree conveniently provided small stone for repairing roads and farm tracks and for filling the centre of dry stone walls. It's hard to imagine a railway steam engine chuffing through the car park pulling a line of carriages crammed with people, and heading up the valley, but in 1884 two brothers, Ambrose and Charles Miller, formed 'The Ennerdale Railway Company' and petitioned Parliament for powers to build a railway:-

> *commencing in the parish of Arlecdon and township of Frizington...and terminating in the township of Ennerdale at a certain beck known as "Gillerthwaite Beck"... and to stop up, cross, divert or alter, either temporarily or permanently, all such turnpike and other roads, highways, footways, railways, tramways, waters, watercourses, rivers, streams and becks...and to purchase and take by compulsion, and also by agreement, lands houses, and tenements...for the purpose of the said intended railway*

It was to be a full gauge railway over six miles in length, starting at Arlecdon and entering Ennerdale a short distance above Tom Butt Cottages in the village before cutting across the fields to pass between How Hall farm and the Anglers Inn. A station was to be built for the convenience of the Inn. The proposal was then to take the line between Routen Farm and Mireside Farm, skirt round the foot of Bowness Knott and then, maintaining the same height above the lake, push up the valley to terminate at Gillerthwaite. Presenting their case for a railway, the promoters argued that it was needed to develop the mineral rights of the valley and that there were large tracts on both sides of the lake which were lying idle on account of their inaccessibility. A spokesman for the company said that 100,000 was not an extravagant estimate of the number of people who would benefit from having a railway in the valley and it was clear from the company's prospectus that they planned to have first, second and third class carriages for passengers and were prepared to carry ore from the mines, coal, manure, limestone, farm animals, parcels and in fact anything to make the railway profitable. Mr David Ainsworth, whose family owned the Bleach Works and a large amount of land in Ennerdale, argued that there was no public necessity whatever for the line and it was a speculative proposition. His view was supported by Canon Rawnsley who, fourteen years later, was one of the founders of the National Trust. He voiced his strong opposition to the railway before a Select Committee in London, and though an appeal went to the House of Lords, it was defeated. Had the building of the railway gone ahead, and had it survived to the present day, not only would it have been a memorable journey for locals and visitors alike, it would have overcome the problem of transporting timber out of the forest. But at what cost to the peace and immeasurable beauty of this remote valley?

Ennerdale Hall

Demolished during the expansion of Rowrah Quarry

the forest ......

When the Forestry Commission was formed after the 1914-18 war with orders to acquire land and plant trees to build up a strategic reserve of timber, the Lake District valleys were a prime target. On the 31st of March 1925, a wordy legal document was 'signed, sealed and delivered' in London by representatives of the Earl of Lonsdale and by the Secretary of the Forestry Commission; and for £2,000 the Forestry Commission became the owner of five hundred Herdwick sheep and *'2716 acres, or thereabouts, situate at Ennerdale Dale Head... subject to a tenancy held by James Williamson and Joseph Yates Williamson of Routen Farm.'* Perhaps in the hope of a revival of the prosperous days of mining in Ennerdale, the noble Lord retained the mineral rights.

The area acquired by the Commission reached from Great Gable, by Haystacks and Scarth Gap Pass, to High Stile on the north side of the valley, and by Kirk Fell and Black Sail Pass to Pillar on the south side. The foresters were intent on planting the lot with conifers, but the fierce resistance of mother nature above the 1500ft contour (457 mtrs), and the objections of influential preservationists below it, forced a change of plan, and the tree line was kept low and confined within a natural boundary formed by the old drove roads of Black Sail and Scarth Gap

Whether it was with the attraction of a cheque book or the threat of a compulsory purchase order is not known, but in their quest for land further down the valley the Commission persuaded several other owners to sell their land, including John Tyson, a Yeoman farmer of Far Moor End Farm. On the 11th of August 1926, in return for the sum of £6,750, he parted with the farms of High Gillerthwaite and Low Gillerthwaite; 3,830 acres of land and 1,119 Herdwick sheep. Including payments of smaller sums paid to other landowners, the Forestry Commission became the owners of nearly 8,000 acres in one of the most attractive valleys in the Lake District for a little over £10,000.

There was a deluge of criticism, and considerable alarm that this relatively forgotten and untouched valley might be ruined. A columnist in the Whitehaven News wrote :-

> *The glamour of the dale is too sacred to be broken; it is something too wonderful than to be gained by the mere perfunctory visit of inquisitive motors. It takes a man to the primitive pleasures of wide and elusive visions, the breath of mountain winds with all the natural joys of tramping through the bracken, the gorse and the purple heather.*

But in a reply to the paper Dr R.H. Quine was more pragmatic:-

> *Apart from the value to the nation of these forests the result of this work will (in a score of years or so) be a great addition to the beauty and seclusion of the dale without in the least destroying its remote tranquility. It will enhance enormously its value as a sanctuary for man, birds, beasts and fishes.*

In the Manchester Guardian a writer, having vented his anxiety, conceded that the impact of afforestation might not be as bad as he thought and he went on:-

> *Ennerdale, the wildest dale head in the Lakes, may have a slightly different aspect, but it should be at least as beautiful and as wild as it is now, and the added cover of the birds should restore a particular charm in which it has not been rich of late. Lord Lonsdale's*

young Shetland ponies have been a pleasant figure in the Ennerdale landscape, but they do not sing.

It was to be a long time before the Commission reared anything tall enough for a bird to perch on and sing, but the Foresters got on with the job in hand and the first trees were planted near High Beck, below Pillar, in 1926.

A proposal to build seven houses for forestry workers and their families at Gillerthwaite was modified and in the end only four were built, two bungalows for workers and two houses for a forester and a foreman. To fence the entire boundary line of the forest, the forestry workers had to laboriously dig paths up the sides of the fells, then carry the rolls of wire and fence posts on their backs. Later the task was made easier when an enterprising forestry worker who lived at Gillerthwaite bought a mule and hired it to the Commission. It was also used to carry bags of young trees up the fells ready for planting. The working conditions of the men were particularly arduous and the pay very poor. One retired forestry worker who planted some of the first trees in Ennerdale said to me, "No matter how tired and weary you were at the end of the day, the wages were that low you still had the strength to carry your pay packet home!" If bad weather prevented the men from working, they did not get paid. Some men cycled 11 miles each day from Cleator Moor, often to be told there was no work for them that day. When King George V died in 1936, the men were given the day of the funeral off as a mark of respect; but were told that if it rained on the day they would not be able to work anyway, so they would not get paid. Fortunately the day of the funeral was fine and the men got their pay! On another occasion, one of the men collapsed and died while digging drains below Pillar Rock and his workmates carried him the three miles down to Gillerthwaite on an improvised stretcher. The forester told them to carry the body into the man's house then return to work and finish the drain.

The iron heart of authority did soften slightly when, in August 1937, Sharp, the foreman who lived at Gillerthwaite, put up a strong case for being allowed the use of an official motor vehicle, *'as the journey to Blengdale and Lowther Park areas was quite an ordeal in the winter, as well as time being lost, if done on a push cycle.'* The unfortunate man explained he had to bike all the way from Gillerthwaite and over the Cold Fell road in all weathers to supervise men in Blengdale Forest at Gosforth, a round trip of 40 miles. The occasional use of a Forestry Commission vehicle was granted!

Concerned that public access to forests would result in forest fires, the Forestry Commission adopted a strict locked-gate 'keep out' policy in its new plantations; but with several public footpaths and an ancient drove road running through Ennerdale, the Commission was obliged to acknowledge rights of way and, in November 1937, issued instructions that a stile should be built wherever a path crossed a fence. Mindful of the fire risk, the Commission Chairman made arrangements with the Youth Hostels Association to assist in providing fire patrols in the valley, and for YHA members staying at Black Sail Hostel to be trained in the use of fire-fighting equipment.

By the mid 1940s it was clear that the old drove road from Bowness Knott to the head of the valley was hopelessly inadequate for the regular passage of motor vehicles, and the Commission's proposal to widen and resurface it sparked off a full-scale confrontation with the Friends of the Lake District, who feared that it would open the valley to motorists. The thorny subject of the 'Ennerdale Road' was frequently raised in Parliament and led to lively exchanges of opinion but, with the Government on their side, the Forestry Commission won the day. The improvement scheme, costing £55,000, was completed in 1948 and it prompted a writer in the newsletter of the Friends of the Lake District to comment sarcastically, *'Some day therefore, but not yet, the great timbers of Ennerdale - weighty as the pyramids and (for so we must suppose if ends are to meet when the account is cast up) saleable in the market at a price rivalling the wealth of fabled Croesus - will come forth in majesty down the road.'*

Having won the fight to improve the road up the valley from Bowness Knott, the Forestry Commission Chairman, Lord Robinson, began looking ahead to the time when heavy vehicles would have to transport mature timber out of the forest to Ennerdale Bridge and beyond. In July 1949 he announced that *'negotiations should be made with a view to following the existing lake margin road - the most direct and reasonable route for development.'* This route, following the lake edge past the Anglers Inn and out by Sawdust Lonning, was almost as sacred to the preservationists as was the drove road up the valley. There must have been some intensive lobbying behind the scenes, for the scheme was quietly dropped and the matter not raised again until Cumberland County Council took the initiative in the 1950s with plans to widen the narrow road past Routen Farm. Several landowners were involved, and to go ahead with the scheme the County Council had to acquire the land by compulsory purchase in one transaction; but J.S.R. Chard, the Head of the Forestry Commission in the north of England, was strangely unco-operative. At a meeting on the 8th of September 1958 he declared, "The estimation of the yield of timber from Ennerdale will hardly justify any additional bridges or roads to those already planned." Except for two short sections the road was never widened, and present-day 30 ton timber-laden juggernauts have great difficulty negotiating a lane designed for the horse and cart.

The Forestry Commission has been criticised heavily over the years for planting 'rows and rows of boring conifers,' and ornithologists and naturalists complained that the forests would be 'sterile', but visitors to the valley will soon realise that these concerns were unfounded. The mistakes of the post war rush to build up a strategic resource of timber have been remedied, and today's foresters are acutely aware that, in environmentally sensitive areas, commercial woodland has to fit comfortably into the landscape. Considerable effort has been made to exclude sheep from the forest and, as a result of the growth of vegetation, wild flowers are prolific, butterflies are common and mammal and bird life is rich . Roe deer and buzzards are seen regularly, and the forest has a thriving colony of red squirrels.

Look upon the forest as a large farm which, instead of growing food, grows trees. Like any other farmer's crop, the trees are harvested and then the ground replanted. On average, each piece of woodland in the forest is visited, and the growth inspected by the Forester, every five years from the age of twenty five to when the woodland is finally clear-felled at around fifty to sixty five years old. In some areas trees are allowed to grow until past old age for their recreation, conservation and landscape value. As you travel round the forest you will see stacks of logs by the roadside, some of which are marked with green paint and others with red. This denotes the quality of the timber. Green is top quality and is transported to sawmills at Carlisle, Dumfries and Ayrshire where it is sawn into lengths suitable for the building trade. Red is poorer quality and, according to its grade, goes for packing timber, such as pallets. Smaller diameter timber, i.e. the top of the tree, goes to a mill at Workington where it is pulped for the manufacture of toiletry packaging, chocolate boxes and similar products, or is sent to a factory in North Wales which manufactures chip board for making furniture.

The predominant tree in the forest is the much-maligned Sitka Spruce. It is a 'grow anywhere' tree, and for that reason there are a lot of them about. It is easily recognised by the blue / grey sheen of its foliage and scaly bark, and if you grab hold of the foliage you will have a first hand experience of pine 'needles'. The Norway Spruce is green, has a smooth, rather orange-coloured bark, and the foliage is soft to hold. This is the popular 'Christmas' tree. Other 'commercial' trees to be seen are Scots Pine, Corsican Pine, and Hybrid Larch. There are Beech, Mountain Ash, Birch and Oak, including, near Gillerthwaite, the lovely American Oak which turns a gorgeous red in the Autumn. Identifying trees is great fun; take a book with you.

A map of the forest, showing the forest trails, is available from Whinlatter Visitor Centre, in Whinlatter Forest, near Keswick. A book describing walks in and around the valley is available from Ennerdale Bridge shop.

In the late 1980s the Government divided the Forestry Commission into two separate bodies, Forest Enterprise and the Forestry Authority. Forest Enterprise is responsible for planting, harvesting and marketing, and also recreation and wildlife in the forests, while the Forestry Authority is a regulatory body which ensures that forests, whether public or privately owned, are properly managed.

Gillerthwaite Bridge

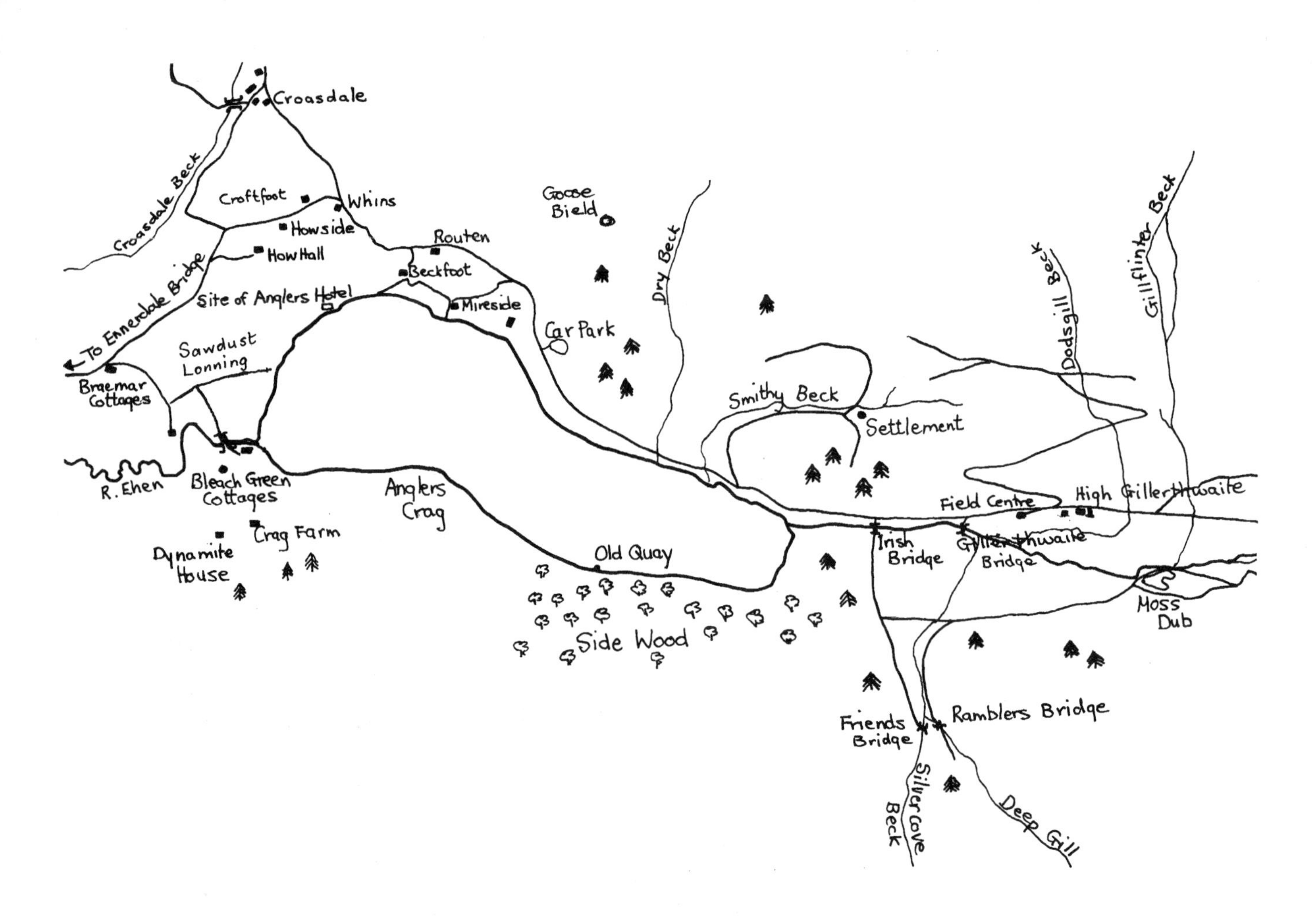
Croasdale
Croasdale Beck
Croftfoot
Whins
Howside
How Hall
To Ennerdale Bridge
Site of Anglers Hotel
Routen
Beckfoot
Mireside
Goose Bield
Dry Beck
Car Park
Sawdust Lonning
Braemar Cottages
R. Ehen
Bleach Green Cottages
Anglers Crag
Crag Farm
Dynamite House
Old Quay
Side Wood
Smithy Beck
Settlement
Dodsgill Beck
Gillflinter Beck
Field Centre
High Gillerthwaite
Irish Bridge
Gillerthwaite Bridge
Moss Dub
Friends Bridge
Ramblers Bridge
Silver Cove Beck
Deep Gill

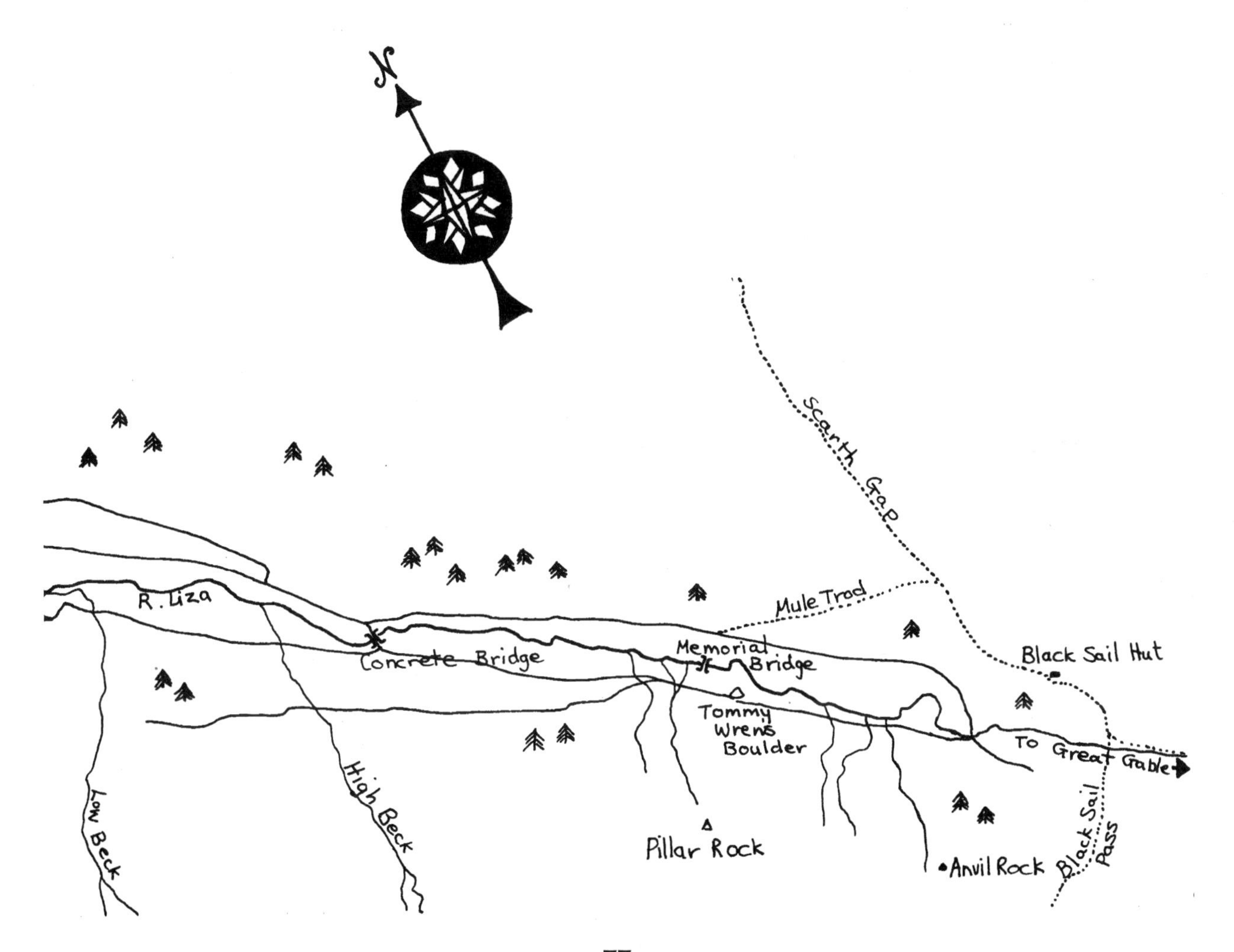
N
Scarth Gap
Mule Trod
R. Liza
Concrete Bridge
Memorial Bridge
Black Sail Hut
Tommy Wren's Boulder
To Great Gable
Low Beck
High Beck
Pillar Rock
Anvil Rock
Black Sail Pass

A guided tour ......

Leaving the car park on what was once an old drove road linking Ennerdale with Buttermere and Wasdale, the forest road descends down Hause Brow to the edge of the lake and along to an attractive wooded peninsula with a tiny horseshoe-shaped bay. This is Clay Dub, better known to local folk as Tadpole Dub. Just beyond the Dub is the start of the Forestry Commission's Smithy Beck Trail, and close to this spot there were once three almost perfectly round boulders which the local men used for weightlifting contests. The smaller one of the three was called the 'Lady's Stone', the middle one the 'Man's Stone' and the larger one, weighing over two hundredweight (101 kilos), was called the 'Strong Man's Stone'. Unfortunately the stones were lost during road-widening operations in 1948. Continuing on, the road crosses a concrete bridge over Smithy Beck, not much to look at compared to the roaring torrent it is when pouring down a deep gorge higher up the fell; but every year in mid-November it becomes the focus of attention for scientists when thousands of Char come up from the depths of the lake to spawn in the gravel beds. It is an incredible sight and one of the wonders of nature.

Leaving Smithy Beck the road swings round the bay to a branch road that climbs up to Smithy Beck Settlement. The settlement is an interesting group of medieval ruins believed to have been the dwellings of people who smelted iron ore using the native oak woods to make charcoal. The settlement is well worth a visit, and information boards on the site provide details of its history. Back at the lake edge, the road skirts the foot of a hill called Latterbarrow, its lower slopes covered with survivors of the ancient oak forest which, fortunately, were probably too difficult for the charcoal burners to reach. Immediately below Latterbarrow, the final stretch of the River Liza runs smooth and placid before it enters the lake at an attractive delta, a regular feeding spot for chattering Mallard ducks and the solitary Heron. This is Char Dub, another favourite spawning place of that mysterious fish, where every year scientists set nets to catch them and water bailiffs set traps to catch poachers intent on emptying the nets. The Foresters have gone to a lot of trouble to build a footpath along the river bank so, if you are walking, please stay on it. If cycling or on a horse keep on the road, both routes eventually reach a concrete causeway crossing the river. In official jargon it is a 'Piped Ford,' but it is more commonly known as the 'Irish Bridge,' and was built in the 1980s to provide vehicular access to the forests on the south side of the river. There is a popular swimming pool downstream of the bridge.

From the Irish Bridge there is a good view of Great Cove, topped by Haycock, on the left, and Silver Cove, crowned by Caw Fell, on the right. Leaving the Irish Bridge, the road climbs a hill known as Red Bank and there are wide views across the valley. Though now part of the forest footpath network, the narrow wooden bridge over the river was not built for the benefit of walkers, but to enable farmers at Gillerthwaite to move sheep back and forth from the fells. At the crest of the hill there is another remnant of the oak forest, and beyond it the road runs by a plantation of tall European Larch. This type of Larch is noted for its resistance to rot and, although the poet Wordsworth was very dismissive of Larch plantations, likening them to *'a sort of abominable vegetable manufactory'*, it was the countryman's favourite timber for making gates, posts and rails. Sadly, it has been ousted by advancements in the chemical treatment of Spruce and other softwoods and is now rarely planted in commercial forests.

The collection of buildings below the Larch trees is Low Gillerthwaite Field Centre, once Low Gillerthwaite Farm, and a little further on is Gillerthwaite Youth Hostel with High Gillerthwaite Farm next to it.

Gillerthwaite ......

An 18th century traveller in Lakeland commented that:-

> *Gillerthwaite is a narrow tract of cultivated land, a peninsula on the lake...where the mountains are barren in the extreme...This little spot has two cottages upon it and has no neighbouring habitations...On the whole there is something melancholy in this scenery, and the mind is apt to be depressed rather than enlivened and touched with pleasure...*

It is believed that, in the 16th century, there were four tenements at Gillerthwaite; but while there are records and eye-witness accounts of two farms at High Gillerthwaite, where the others were is not clear. In 1609 William Roger, William Bowman, Anthony Fletcher and Richard Littledale, all of Gillerthwaite, were heavily fined for keeping dogs to hunt deer. They had been fined in 1604 for 'currying' leather, so it appears they had a useful income from poaching the Lord of the Manor's deer and making leather from the skins. Another family who fell foul of the law for poaching deer were the Sharpes, and church registers show that 'Nicholas Sharpe of Gillathwaite was buried on 16th of October 1654' and 'Katherin Sharpe of Gillathwaite was baptised in April 1677'.

In the 17th century there were certainly two small farms very close together in the yard of the present-day High Gillerthwaite Farm. Fortunately one of them has survived, but the other was pulled down towards the end of the 19th century. In 1829 they were occupied by Isaac Sharp and John Kirkhaugh who, like their predecessors, were in trouble with the Lord of the Manor for helping themselves to his deer. But, as one traveller of the time observed, the two farms at Gillerthwaite were brought almost to the point of starvation by deer raiding the crops. In desperation, the farmers ringed their fields with hay forks, scythe blades and bits of sharp metal. When the deer jumped into the fields they were impaled and no doubt ended up on the farmer's dinner table.

By 1841 the two farms at High Gillerthwaite had merged into one, and another farm was in occupation at Low Gillerthwaite. Though very probably it was on the site of an earlier dwelling I have not found any reference to Low Gillerthwaite in old documents.

In 1841 High Gillerthwaite was occupied by:-

John Tyson	age 50	Sarah Tyson	age 40
William Tyson	age 20	Jane Tyson	age 15
George Tyson	age 14	Daniel Tyson	age 9

Low Gillerthwaite was occupied by:-

John Colebank	age 30	Hanah Colebank	age 30
Margaret Colebank	age 2	John Harrington	age 20 (Servant)
Bridget Porter	age 50	Dinah Jackson	age 15 (Servant)

Low Gillerthwaite

Ten years later, records show that the Colebanks had gone and John Tyson was now the owner of both High and Low Gillerthwaite, a combined total of 110 acres (44 hectares), a huge farm in those days. The family moved into Low Gillerthwaite and the buildings at High Gillerthwaite were left to crumble. Like so many of their kind, the farming families were very hospitable, and when Dr David Lietch called at Low Gillerthwaite with two friends in November 1850 they sat down to:-

> *an immense platter of baked flesh and a mountainous pile of mashed potatoes...while in the metal pan on the fire, covered with a metal lid on which was heaped red embers forming the usual oven of the mountains, the mighty remains of an apple pie being heated up. Cheese upon the upper shelves near to the rafters, and hooks for hanging goodly supplies of bacon...a fireplace ornamented with circular projections of stones, whereupon to deposit kettles or pans, and a crew of shepherds dogs lying about the stone floor*

Low Gillerthwaite was also known as one of the finest Herdwick sheep farms in the Lake District, carrying in the region of 3,000 sheep. During the tenancy of the Birkett family at the turn of the 19th century and up to the 1930s, the farm was renowned for breeding top-quality Herdwick rams. The purchase of High and Low Gillerthwaite from the Tyson family by the Forestry Commission in 1926 effectively made Low Gillerthwaite farm unworkable, and after a year or two the Birketts sold off most of their sheep and left. Much of the land was let to a neighbouring farmer. For some years the house and some land was tenanted by Mr and Mrs Stan Hughes who, in 1942, also used some of the buildings as a youth hostel on behalf of the Youth Hostels Association, and their kindness and hospitality became a legend. Stan and his wife were the wardens of Low Gillerthwaite hostel for over twenty five years.

Sheep Shearing at Ennerdale

During the last fortnight hundreds of the hardy mountain sheep in the Ennerdale district have been undergoing their annual shearing. On Wednesday week, Mr Birkett of Gillerthwaite, held one of the old fashioned, though still popular, sheep clippings, when they had the assistance of Messrs J. Bateman and T. Potter, Croasdale; J. and J. Birkett, How Hall; H. Mitchell, Stowbank; W. Rawling, Hollins; J.M. Wallace and J. Ullock, Ennerdale; J. Raven, Fell End; W. Robinson and J. Tyson, Moor End; W.M. Park, Crag Farm; J. Pearson, Whins; W.Muncaster, Mireside; H. Williamson, Routen; J. Smith, Hawes; W. Mulley, Anglers Inn; W. Tinnion, How Hall; R. Kendall and A. Southward, Croasdale. Beautiful weather favoured the occasion and the work was completed in good time. The wants of the workers were admirably attended to by Mrs Wilson Birkett, Miss Birkett, How Hall; Mrs Bateman, Croasdale; Miss Rawling, Hollins; and Mrs Robinson, Moor End.

Whitehaven News 31 October 1911

The arrival of the Forestry Commission in the 1920s also had a lasting impact on High Gillerthwaite. A plan to build seven cottages was modified to two bungalows for workers and two superior houses, one of which was for the forester and the other for the foreman. The old High Gillerthwaite farmhouse was used for storage and the forester's office, and later as a stable for the mule which carried fencing materials and plants up the fell. The original 30 acres (11 hectares) of land belonging to High Gillerthwaite farm was divided into four agricultural holdings assigned to the occupants of the houses, but there were complaints that the forester grabbed the best land and the workers were left to make what they could of the boggy areas! The bungalows and houses were given names; Dodsgill was nearest to the old farmhouse and Lingmell was next door. The houses were known as Starling Dodd (nearest to the bungalows, and the forester's house), and Cat Bell. The first forester was a man of German descent called Stanley Phelps, and

High Gillerthwaite Farmhouse

Gillerthwaite Youth Hostel

John Wren and his wife Mary Ellen and four sons John, William, James and Tom, were the first tenants of Dodsgill. Joe Garbutt, who later died while digging drains below Pillar, moved into Lingmell some time later. The Wrens were an enterprising family and, apart from catering for Bed and Breakfast guests, Mrs Wren baked bread for Black Sail youth hostel and took it up the valley in a pony and trap. She also used the pony and trap to collect the Forestry Commission's tree plants from Arlecdon railway station 6 miles (10 Kilometres) away. The men were equally industrious and, after a hard day working for the Commission, they tended their land, ploughing with a horse and single-furrow plough and growing what they could to eke out their meagre wages. They kept a milk cow and hens, ducks, geese and a pig. Perhaps having spotted a business opportunity, John Wren senior bought a mule from Muncaster Estate at Ravenglass for £2-10-0 (£2-50p) and hired it to the Commission for carrying fencing materials and plants up the fells. When the then Chairman of the Forestry Commission, Lord Robinson, came to Ennerdale on his annual visit to inspect progress, it was the Wren's pony and trap, suitably cleaned and polished and driven by young Tommy Wren, his hair flattened down with water and wearing his best suit, which was hired to convey him up the valley. John Wren and his sons, along with other forestry workers, built a suspension bridge across the Liza just below Gillerthwaite to save a long walk round when working on the opposite side of the river. It remained there for several years until, in a memo to his boss in the 1940s, the forester complained that local children indulged in the dangerous practice of trying to shake each other off it, and shortly afterwards it was removed. The Wren family left Gillerthwaite in 1939, and though for another twenty years the houses were occupied by various other tenants, the beauty of the scenery was no match for the attraction of the convenience of the new forestry workers' houses built at Ennerdale Bridge in the 1950s. After a period lying empty, Lingmell and Dodsgill were let as holiday homes and, for a time, Starling Dodd and Cat Bell were used by a mountaineering club. In 1969 the Youth Hostels Association, keen to fill the gap left by the closure of Low Gillerthwaite hostel, took Starling Dodd and Cat Bell on a long lease and joined them together to make a hostel. The building is likely to remain a youth hostel for the foreseeable future. Meantime, following

Mrs. Wren

Dodsgill Farm,
Gillerthwaite,
Ennerdale,
Cleator.

Terms : 25/- per week.
Supper, Bed & Breakfast, 3/6

the departure of Stan Hughes and his wife from Low Gillerthwaite, the house and buildings were leased to the City of Leeds College Diamond Jubilee Association, and in 1968 the Low Gillerthwaite Field Centre was opened to provide a base, under the supervision of a resident Warden, where school parties and others could attend courses or simply enjoy the countryside.

In 1976, while on a journey around the Lake District on horseback, I happened to pass High Gillerthwaite and was immediately captivated by the remote and very beautiful setting. In 1977, with the intention of running it as a small farm, I was granted the lease of Dodsgill Cottage and ten acres (4 Hectares) of land. When Lingmell became vacant I converted the two cottages into one house, and about the same time the ten acres was increased to thirty.

The roof of the old farmhouse had fallen in and the building was in a derelict state. With the approval of the Forestry Commission I renovated it, taking care to retain its character, and it has since been in use providing basic accommodation for climbers and walkers. During the renovation, a metal box was concealed inside the walls containing the names of the people who helped with the work, the tenants of High and Low Gillerthwaite, several coins, and a list of information which might be useful to a future archaeologist.

On the side of the road by High Gillerthwaite there was an ancient potash kiln in which the farmers of Gillerthwaite burnt bracken to make a soap used for washing sheep. Regrettably the kiln was destroyed in the 1980s by a mechanical digger during forestry draining operations.

The hamlet of Gillerthwaite may be very old, but in 1993 David Kerr, the then forester in charge of Ennerdale, began to take an interest in several large circular mounds he had discovered amongst the trees beyond Gillerthwaite and he asked the National Park's archaeologist to investigate them.

It was found that he had stumbled on not just one but several very ancient settlements. Together they must have housed a large number of people who probably survived on primitive agriculture and from hunting wild animals in the oak forest, but who they were and what happened to them will take some time to establish. At the time of writing, a team of archaeologists from Lancaster University have just completed their third year of survey work, during which they have identified many new features of interest which show that Ennerdale was a well-populated and busy valley many centuries ago.

Of the sites to be seen, a large circle is to be found in the trees, just over the cattle grid beyond Gillerthwaite and opposite the entrance to a forest track, called Gilflinter Road; but the most intriguing of the group, a large circular fort with turf walls and identifiable entrances, is further along the road. After the road crosses a swift-flowing beck, Gilflinter Beck, it drops down and runs level for a distance. Just before it starts to climb a short hill, turn left into the trees and you will soon find the fort.

Continuing up the valley, the landscape becomes very rugged with Pillar, Black Crag and Steeple dominating the skyline, and there is a good view-point at a junction where Gilflinter Road, having run parallel high on the left, emerges onto the forest road. If you want to observe red squirrels Gilflinter Road is the ideal place, but tread quietly and leave your dog at home!

Beyond the junction with Gilflinter Road the forest road dips slightly then levels out, and on the right, hidden by trees, there used to be a wooden footbridge which rotted away in the 1950s. Though pressure was put on the Forestry Commission to re-instate the bridge, they declined to take responsibility for it and in 1956 built a substantial concrete bridge further upstream designed to carry heavy vehicles, but also handy for walkers. The bridge is easily reached at a junction a little further along the road. The right fork, signposted 'Pillar', drops down to the bridge, but ignore it and take the left fork signposted 'Black Sail'.

A short distance along the road, on the right, The British Trust for Conservation Volunteers have rebuilt what is believed to be an ancient sheepfold. A large number of stone sheepfolds are to be found in the valley, often with intriguing shapes, some round, some rectangular and other shaped like an arrow. They are often to be found by the edge of the Liza or the smaller becks where there would be a plentiful supply of water, essential for the old fashioned methods of cleaning and marking the sheep. Many of the folds have been used and maintained in living memory by the Ennerdale shepherds, but were abandoned when the lower valley sheep grazing was lost to afforestation.

The forest road climbs steadily towards the head of the valley and there is a tremendous view of Pillar Rock on the right. Rearing above the valley, it terrified some of the first travellers in Lakeland. Describing the rock in 1795 a visitor wrote :-

> *Frightening would be the vision to the timid, or those unaccustomed to sights like these, and awful to all men if instantaneously transported from even meadows to such rugged uplands, particularly as seen immediately above the path where the rocks are like huge towers falling from immense fortifications*

For generations the superstitious shepherds of Ennerdale went in fear of the rock, believing that it was the home of some evil power. Seen on a dull, wet day when its jagged summit pierces through black storm clouds and streamers of grey mist swirl around the forbidding walls and gullies like demented ghosts, it is easy to understand why rustic countryfolk gave it a wide berth.

But having terrified the Ennerdale folk for so long, it is pleasing that the first ascent of the Rock was made by a local farmer rather than one of the well-to-do academics who some years later were to go down in history as the pioneers of Lakeland rock-climbing.

Pillar Rock was first climbed by John Atkinson of Croftfoot, Ennerdale and the Cumberland Paquet reported on Tuesday July 25th 1826:-

On the 9th inst. Mr John Atkinson of Croftfoot, in Ennerdale, succeeded in attaining the summit of the rock called the Pillar Stone, and although the undertaking has been attempted by thousands before him, it was always relinquished as hopeless; John is therefore the first human being "whose foot has pressed the tender grass" upon this huge pile. His dog, the faithful attendant of the shepherd, lay by his staff at the bottom, and as if conscious of the danger his master was incurring by the attempt, uttered the most piteous cries during his absence. The only precaution he took for his descent was placing pieces of moss on the track by which he ascended. On the top he found several plants of the Juniper tree, some of which he removed and has since planted in the more genial clime of Croftfoot

The route John Atkinson took is now a popular rock climb called the 'Old West Route' - to the right of the rock as you look at it - and what is all the more remarkable about his epic climb is that he was 52 years of age at the time. Many accounts of his feat wrongly describe him as a cooper, but he was a prosperous farmer. The Atkinsons owned Croftfoot and several other farms as well. It was his elder brother Joseph who was a cooper and rake-maker. His younger brother, Jeremiah, was a Minister, and for twenty nine years was the vicar of

Loweswater. The first lady climbers to conquer Pillar Rock were a party led by Miss Barker of Gosforth in 1870.

Many visitors to Ennerdale, including the poet William Wordsworth, have been confused by the names Pillar and Pillar Rock, but they are quite distinct. 'Pillar' is Pillar Fell with a height of 2927 feet (892 mtrs) and 'Pillar Rock' is the impressive pinnacle a few hundred feet high attached to the northern face of Pillar Fell like the figurehead of a giant ship.

A path signposted 'Pillar' drops down to the 'Memorial Bridge', a wooden footbridge over the river built by the Fell and Rock Climbing Club of the Lake District, with help from Cumberland County Council, in memory of members who fell in the 1939-45 war. It was built at this point on the river to enable climbers who had walked over Scarth Gap Pass from Buttermere to reach the rock without having to make a long detour. This walk is made all the easier by a path, signposted 'Scarth Gap'on the Ennerdale side, which starts on the left a short distance along the forest road beyond the footbridge and traverses diagonally up the fellside to Scarth Gap Pass. This is no ordinary walkers' path. It is known as the 'Mule Trod' and was laboriously dug out with picks and shovels by forestry workers in 1926 to enable John Wren's mule to carry fencing materials and plants to the forest boundary.

Anvil Rock

Before continuing along the forest road, enjoy the marvellous view of the fells at the head of the valley. On the left is Green Gable, dropping down to Windy

Gap then rising again to the flat-topped summit of Great Gable. There is a ledge on the craggy face of Great Gable where, until a few years ago, there were the remains of a small stone hut used by smugglers in days gone by to store Wad (Black Lead) stolen from a mine at Seathwaite, in Borrowdale. Resist the temptation to go and look for it; it is a rock-climbing feat! If you like pottering about old mine workings, Dubs Quarry, some distance further along the forest road, is worth seeking out. Visibility permitting, 'Anvil Rock', seen on the skyline high on the right, is a good pointer, so keep a sharp look out for it as you move along the road. It will suddenly appear, admittedly not very large, but a definite anvil shape on the skyline, and just as you see it there should be a beck on your left running under the road. In 1997 a stone at the side of the road was marked with a blue arrow. Follow the beck up the fell to the abandoned buildings of the quarry.

In a report on the quarry dated September 20th 1809, a mining engineer wrote that fresh attempts were being made to bore for slate and large blocks had been found:-

> *but when the workmen attempt to rive them they split into very small pieces due to a great quantity of Flint running thro' the blocks. If the Flint leaves the Vein it will be very profitable, being the best Vein in the Country for Colour, Thickness, and Evenness of Surface, and working very cheap.*

Despite the optimism of the report, there was not enough good slate to develop into a profitable quarry and work seems to have stopped. In his report the engineer mentions evidence of copper in the vicinity of the quarry, but dismissed it as being of poor quality. Someone must have thought it worthwhile digging for and, having had some success, attempts were made to raise capital. In a letter dated 22 February1833, Joseph Robson, a Whitehaven mining engineer writing to a client who had commissioned him to assess the prospects for the copper mine, reported:-

> *The mine is situated on the West side of the High Crag at an elevation of about 1,000 feet above the bed of the Liza, opposite Black Sail and 5 miles from Ennerdale Lake...The present*

miners, 3 of whom are Cornish men, and well versed in copper workings, are most sanguine of success in developing a mine of great Richness...it yields about 5oz of Silver per ton of ore. Although this quantity of Silver will not pay for its extraction, yet the quantity may increase...With Respect to the mode of carriage of the ore, it is proposed by the manager to form an inclined self-acting tramway from the mine to the River Liza, about half a mile in length to where there is sufficient water power. The ore will then be crushed and conveyed by carts to the Lake and thence boated, and finally carted to Whitehaven. I have every reason to *believe the speculation genuine and capable of larger development. The official title of the mine I understand is to be "The Great Cumberland Copper Mountain Mine".*

It was an impressive title, but in the event it turned out that the copper mountain wasn't as great a potential investors were led to believe, and the mine went out of business.

Returning to the road, continue to the forest boundary gate and the start of Scarth Gap Pass. The narrow track ahead leads to Black Sail Hostel, one of the remotest, yet most popular, youth hostels in Britain. Go along the track to the hostel, and since you have now travelled over six miles from Bowness Knott, it's an ideal place to stop to eat your sandwiches and enjoy the solitude of the remote head of the dale. So intent were the YHA on preserving the tranquillity of this unique place, the details for Black Sail Hostel in the YHA Members Handbook for 1934 states, *'The cyclist is not encouraged to obtrude his machine, though he could leave it at Gillerthwaite Farm and tramp the remaining four miles.'*

To shelter men working their sheep, there was a building of sorts and sheep pens at Black Sail for many centuries. The Williamsons of Routen farm had the grazing rights at the head of the dale for a long time, and the late Charles Williamson recalled as a small boy being taken up the valley to Black Sail hut on a horse-drawn cart loaded with shepherds and their dogs and enough food for a week. Being able to clip or dose sheep at the head of the valley saved having to walk them the seven miles to Routen, and the shepherds looked forward to going to Black Sail, they said it was like going on holiday! The hut was a very primitive one-room construction in those days. There was a fireplace where they cooked meals, but no bunks; they all slept on mattresses on the floor. The evenings were spent cracking yarns and singing hunting songs. As sheep farming methods changed, the hut was used less and less until it was finally abandoned and became derelict. In the 1930s it was leased to the Youth Hostels Association who have done a wonderful job of rebuilding it, and it is likely to remain a youth hostel for all time.

Returning to the forest road, turn left and follow it downhill to a ford across the River Liza. Most times it is safe to cross; but after periods of heavy rain it is not recommended, and you are faced with a detour to a footbridge beyond Black Sail Hostel and then by riverside path with several stiles to re-join the forest road on the other side of the ford. Spouting from a tiny spring at the head of the dale below the saddle of Windy Gap, the infant Liza bounces playfully down the fellside gathering pace as she goes, and would probably be nothing more than a spirited youngster all the way to the lake were it not for joining hands with Tongue Beck, Loft Beck, and Sail Beck before she has hardly travelled a mile and a half (2 kilometres). If the weather is fine, the quartet gurgle lazily down the valley, trickling musically over waterfalls and drifting silently through deep pools. But if the weather turns nasty and storm clouds gather, the fickle Liza and her friends fly into a temper and within minutes are roaring down the valley in a raging fury, tearing at trees, snatching at the river bank, smashing down fences and threatening bridges until, having left a trail of destruction six miles long, (9 kilometres,) they sink exhausted into the lake at Char Dub.

If it is safe to cross over the ford, there is a track that shoots off to the left and a few yards along it, until it was destroyed by mindless vandals, there used to be a very useful forest shelter. In February 1964, representatives of the Forestry Commission and the Outward Bound Mountain School in Eskdale met to discuss the possibility of the school building a log cabin in the forest to accommodate lads during mountain activity expeditions. One of the Commission's Directors, J.R. Thom, was particularly enthusiastic about the project and wrote in a memo, *'I do hope that it is possible to come to an arrangement with the Outward Bound School for the erection of a log cabin.'*

Black Sail Hostel

For reasons lost in bureaucracy, the Outward Bound log cabin was never built; but the idea of having a shelter in the forest for walkers and climbers was resurrected in the 1980s when the then forester, Keith Hobson, was instructed to dispose of a wooden shed at Gillerthwaite. The forestry workers had christened it 'Hazel Lodge' and, complete with its smart name board, Keith had Hazel Lodge carted up the valley and rebuilt on the south side of the Liza below Black Sail hostel. For years it gave shelter to countless walkers and saved many a life in winter when Black Sail hostel was closed, but when the yob element found their way into the hills, Hazel Lodge was vandalised until it was beyond repair. All that remains is a sign by the edge of the track with the mournful caption, *'The forest shelter has been removed due to vandalism.'*

Leaving the site of Hazel Lodge, rejoin the forest road, turning left. On the steep fellside ahead there is another zigzag path cut by forestry workers in the 1920s for carrying fencing materials and plants, but it is not easy to find and the best place to view it is from the other side of the valley, high up on Scarth Gap Pass. The road is now heading back down the valley along the foot of Lookingstead, part of the Pillar range, and a tragic event happened in this area in 1876 which is commemorated by a cairn hidden in the trees. On the 14th of August, 1876, a London silversmith set off from Rosthwaite in Borrowdale to walk over Styhead Pass to Wasdale, then by Black Sail Pass to Buttermere in time to catch the afternoon coach to Keswick. It was a very hot day, and when he reached the inn at Wasdale Head he looked weary and was advised to rest. But, worried that he might miss the coach in Buttermere, he refused, and in blistering heat he set off towards Black Sail and was never seen alive again. When he failed to return to his hotel a search party was organised and, though a shepherd and several helpers were engaged to search the head of Ennerdale, they found nothing. In September, almost a full month after he had disappeared, a shepherd stumbled on his body. At the inquest the verdict was that he had died from heat-stroke. A large cairn, about eight feet high, was erected on the spot where the body was found. A bronze plaque bears the inscription:-

> *The body of Edward Barnard of Angel Street and Highbury Grove who was lost in this district August 14 was found on this spot Sept 10th 1876.*

Hazel Lodge

The Forestry Commission have a photograph of Barnard's Cairn on the front of their forest map, though they mistakenly call it 'Barney's Cairn'. At present the monument is well hidden but, if the Commission's tree-felling operations eventually expose it in all its magnificence, vandals will surely destroy it.

Meantime, not wishing to go down in history as the person who revealed the location, I offer this description of how to find Barnard's Cairn:-

Leave the ford with back to Gabel
Down forest road through Spruce you'll travel .
But don't explore each rocky cleft
Lookingstead upon the left,
Where by the edge of roadman's pride
Sits a rock, grass topped and grey on side
And almost facing, in reedy bed
Sits another rock, but this one's red.
Face the fell then climb the side
And you'll reach the spot where Barnard died.

Back on the forest road there is a good view of the opposite side of the valley, with High Stile and Gamlin End sharp against the skyline. The road climbs and then descends past a large glacial boulder on the left and another conical monster further down on the right, which henceforth I shall name 'Tommy Wren's Boulder', in honour of a man dedicated to forestry and who thinks that

Ennerdale is the most wonderful place on earth. Having read the notes on Gillerthwaite, you will recall that Tommy was one of the Wren family who were among the first forest workers to be employed when the Commission acquired Ennerdale. In those days working conditions were tough, and when the men spent months draining and planting the fellside below Pillar, the only shelter they had from the gales and heavy rain was a leaky tarpaulin they tied to the boulder and crouched under. When the tarpaulin eventually disintegrated, Tommy somehow managed to lay his hands on an old hen hut and, to protect it from the fierce weather, it was erected next to the boulder and remained there for many years. At the time of writing, Tommy Wren is in his eighties and still reasonably fit and well. As far as I am aware, he is the only survivor of the original forest gang.

Leaving Tommy Wren's Boulder, the road crosses a bridge and forks right and left. If you have time to spare, the left fork slogs up a steep hill to a viewpoint with a magnificent panorama of the lower valley and the lake. The right fork continues to another junction where the substantial concrete bridge, mentioned on the way up the valley, spans a superb rocky gorge. When the river is in spate the waterfalls are quite spectacular. Do not go over the bridge, but take the left fork and follow it until it climbs to a bridge crossing High Beck. The wood on the right just after High Beck is where forestry worker Joe Garbutt died while digging drains in 1927. His workmates built a cairn in his memory, but it was bulldozed away during later road-widening operations.

Tommy Wren's Boulder

The lovely waterfalls of High Beck may inspire you to

Moss Dub

poetry, but are nothing like as awe-inspiring as the cascades of Low Beck, further down the road at the bottom of the hill. Unfortunately, Low Beck flows down a deep rocky ghyll with sheer sides overhung with trees and the waterfalls are not easy to see. Great care should be taken if venturing into the ghyll or near the edge. In the 1930s the Forestry Commission had plans to build a hydro electricity scheme in the beck to supply the houses and farms at Gillerthwaite, but there were weighty objections and it was dropped. Gillerthwaite still does not have mains electricity.

Past Low Beck, the road swings left in a long curve and starts to climb a hill. At the foot of the hill a narrow track on the right leads to Moss Dub, a shallow pond created by the Forestry Commission to encourage fish and bird life. The Commission provided a wooden hide with observation windows but this was destroyed in 1996 when hooligans set it on fire. The track round Moss Dub joins the forest road again, so turn right and continue along to a gate. Through the gate the road crosses Woundell Beck by a piped ford. The ruins on the right are part of an old farm where, according to elderly local people, there was once a blacksmith's forge. A little way past the ruins, a track on the left is worth venturing along to the spot where the foaming waters of Silver Cove Beck and Deep Gill join together to form Woundell Beck. The forest track soon ends and a narrow path continues on and drops down to two wooden footbridges, one spanning Silver Cove Beck, replacing the original rickety plank on the public footpath, and the other, connecting with the Forestry Commission's network of trails, across Deep Gill. The first bridge, over Silver Cove Beck, known as the Friends' Bridge, was built by the Friends of the Lake District in memory of Mr J.H. Jolly, a former member of the Friends. The second bridge, across Deep Gill, is known as the Ramblers' Bridge. Cumberland County Council contributed £400 of the £1100 needed to build it, and the rest was raised by the Ramblers Association with generous donations from the C.H.A., the Y.H.A., the Camping Club of Great Britain, affiliated clubs and individual members. They were both opened on June 22nd 1974.

Retracing your steps to the forest road, go through the gate and the road leads to the Irish Bridge and the end of the tour through the forest and around the valley. The large field on the right before the bridge is another site that has excited archaeologists but, at the time of writing, has not yet been explored.

Footnote ......

A newspaper report in July 1926 stated that Sir Albert Wyon, a keen supporter of the National Trust, had provided funds for the Trust to purchase from the Forestry Commission between 3,000 and 4,000 acres of land (1115 and 1620 hectares) at the head of Ennerdale valley. It seems, however, that the Commission must have decided against the sale for, in a document dated 7th of June 1927, the Forestry Commission leased all the land above the forest planting boundary to the National Trust for a period of 500 years at an annual rent of £1. The ownership of Black Sail hostel was retained by the Commission. One of the provisos of the lease was that the land could be taken back at any time into the possession of the Forestry Commission, and this right was exercised in 1981 when two small areas of land on Lingmell were taken back as part of the Commission's 'Ennerdale Plan.' In 1991, following a claim by a private landowner, it was confirmed that the well-known Innominate Tarn on Haystacks was owned by the Forestry Commission. Innominate Tarn and the straggling summit of Haystacks were favourite places of that incomparable guide book writer the late A. Wainwright. In 1965 he wrote:-

> *Afforestation in Ennerdale has cloaked the lower slopes...in a dark and funereal shroud of foreign trees, an intrusion that nobody who knew Ennerdale of old can ever forgive, the former charm of the valley having been destroyed*

When he died, Wainwright's ashes were scattered on Haystacks and as he looks down on Ennerdale from his high seat, hopefully he will approve of the sensitive approach that is being made to integrate afforestation into the landscape. The Ennerdale valley has seen many changes in its long history but it has lost none of its charm, its rugged beauty or the peace and tranquillity that have attracted generations of visitors to its lonely fells.